NET-ORIENTED EDUCATION

NET-ORIENTED EDUCATION

B.M. SHARMA

AKANSHA PUBLISHING HOUSE
NEW DELHI-110059 (INDIA)

AKANSHA PUBLISHING HOUSE
R 37-B, Vani Vihar, Uttam Nagar
New Delhi-110059
Email: ektabooks@yahoo.com
Ph. : 9212065579 / 9811582579

Showroom
4649/21B, Ansari Road
Darya Ganj
New Delhi - 110 002

Net-oriented Education

First Edition 2004
Reprint- 2005
Reprint–2006
Reprint : 2012

PRINTED IN INDIA

Published by M.P. Misra for Akansha Publishing House, New Delhi and Printed at Tarun Offset Press, Delhi.

Preface

Net-oriented education is a popular term for the use of internet technologies to support education. It has been an important area of experimentation within the educational system for the last couple of years, and has become an important area for the business world as well.

It is widely believed that the World Wide Web (WWW) can be a powerful tool to enfranchise under-served learners via interactive learning and online support through a virtual community with a cultural sense of belonging. By gaining access to anywhere-anytime learning opportunities for completing a post-secondary education and getting workforce training, students will be prepared to make greater contributions in the knowledge society.

Net-oriented education is not a technology. It is an emerging model of learning at a distance through a diversity of information and communication resources, and through mediated human interaction. Net-oriented-learning entails a knowledge-construction process resulting from the interactions of learners with instructors and other learners, through computer communication, and with distributed information resources accessible from anywhere through the Web's hypertext interconnections. Careful instructional design with a constructivist view and assessment methodologies will insure the highest quality levels of online learning.

The issues and opportunities of net-oriented education is comprehensively discussed in the present volume. It will be a highly beneficial reference tool for students, teachers, academicians and policy makers of the cyber age.

Editor

Contents

	Preface	*v*
1.	Influence of Globalisation on Education	1
2.	Technological Impacts on Education	33
3.	Essentials of Web-based Education	89
4.	Web-based Teaching and Learning	164
5.	World Wide Web—The Boost of Distance Education	212
6.	Costs of Net-oriented Education	261
	Index	293

1

Influence of Globalisation on Education

Globalization has become today's catchword. In debate, it raises passions on all sides. Amongst its more common associations are the growing integration of the world's economies, a lowering of barriers to communication, a growing connection between all segments of society, increase in the speed at which ideas, goods and people move around. Thanks to new technologies of communications and information, massive quantities of data become available almost instantaneously via Internet and other telecommunications media.

Globalization is perceived by many to influence how teaching and learning are conducted. It has major impact on cultural identity and on the capacity to deal with differences. Often globalization is seen as a force driving towards cultural homogenization.

Education is not exempt from the process of globalization. The topic of globalization and its implications for higher education are wide-ranging. There are many dimensions - transnational education, multi-national arrangements governing access, mobility and quality assurance. All link to globalization.

Globalization influences quality assurance, accreditation and the recognition of qualifications - especially when they are earned through transnational education. It is in this domain that some argue for putting international frameworks in place to regulate quality assurance, accreditation and the recognition of diplomas.

Amongst the promises that some people believe globalization can fulfil is the provision of equal access to higher education and narrowing the gap between developed and developing countries. Others argue quite the opposite.

Still, another aspect of globalization is much feared. It is the commodification of higher education. The General Agreement on Trade in Services (GATS) with its on-going and forward moving negotiations could change higher education dramatically. Many international education organizations do not agree that education services should figure as part of GATS. Some including IAU signed a Declaration opposing GATS. Proposals for alternative ways to "regulate" international exchange in higher education are now discussed.

Globalization is a challenge to the development of our world. It opens new opportunities. But it also heralds new uncertainties. These ought to be recognized, scrutinized closely and dealt with. Both as observers and actors, higher education institutions and organizations have an important part to play.

With the growing global demand and the possibilities offered by new communications and information technologies, in the context of a "knowledge society" and "lifelong learning", the development of transnational or borderless education has become a subject of debate in the academic community. Transnational education (also referred to as TE or TNE) is not necessarily a new aspect of education however, the magnitude of its global growth is unprecedented. Transnational education is seen as going beyond traditional international academic co-operation and having major implications not only for individual institutions of higher education but also for higher education systems, international organizations, private corporations and "customers" concerned by this type of education.

Even if there are different opinions regarding the meaning of transnational education, the most general definition is :

> "All types of higher education study programmes, or sets of courses of study, or educational services (including those of distance education) in which the learners are located in a country different from the one where the awarding institution is based. Such programmes may belong to the education system of a State different from the State in which it operates, or may operate independently of any national education system."

The challenges of transnational education originate, foremost, from the entry of new private for-profit, virtual, and corporate providers into the domestic and international higher education markets. In addition, the competition they create and their often unregulated status has major implications with regard to the quality assurance of this type of education.

Transnational education is not viewed as threatening by all, nor is it likely to begin to transform overnight the education systems in general and the role of the university in particular. Transnational education is seen as an answer to demands for access where some national systems are not able to respond. For this reason, transnational education tends to develop particularly in countries or regions where there are major gaps between the supply and demand for higher education:

— systems where the supply of higher education is weak; where the selection process is highly restrictive;

— noticeable gaps between programme content and student and/or employer expectations;

— rigid systems, lacking diversification of programmes, no opportunities for learning and working at the same time, or no option for the student to learn in a language of his/her choice.

These limitations make transnational education, which focuses on finding such niche markets, an attractive educational offer.

There are various ways in which transnational education can be organized and/or delivered:

— through various forms of "distance education";

— twinning programs, articulation programs or branch campuses;

— franchising arrangements;

— off-shore institutions;

— international institutions.

This is not, of course, a complete list of forms that transnational education can take but merely its more known manifestations. Indeed, many other initiatives may exist and remain to be assessed in this rapidly evolving field. For a comprehensive discussion and typology of new higher education providers and the questions they raise for quality assurance in particular, please see Robin Middlehurst's article "Quality Assurance - Implications of New Forms of Higher Education".

Transnational education in its wide variety of forms is part of a broader trend of globalization. Higher education institutions, international organizations and national education agencies will need to examine this trend and be aware of the threats and/or opportunities offered by transnational education.

Education in a Globalized World

Before the institution of public education, the education of the elite was carried out by tutors working with their pupils in a highly personalized manner. Education of the mind, of the capacities and talents of the individual, was a basic principle. In a different class context, for children of rural or working families, education or upbringing was also a personal affair, governed by families and local communities. Fitting into a community, whether a local or national culture and way of life, can be seen as the educational imperative cutting across these contexts.

Later, when schooling as a public institution took shape, this notion of local and familial responsibility for upbringing remained. The idea that schools acted *in loco parentis*, and the policy structures that supported community control over schooling, situated the learner in a relation to immediate and familiar learning needs: needs of identity, affiliation, citizenship, and work roles that responded to a context that was already close at hand. Even in more centralized, nationalized public school systems the same dynamic can be seen at work, simply invoked at a different level: policies enforce conformity and identification with a national tradition, a larger community, a broader context of citizenship and work responsibility, but still one in which the conditions of affiliation are based on relative proximity and homogeneity.

The implications of this educational process, especially as it becomes a public concern, go well beyond the aim of developing the individual self. As the economics of education tell us, the education of the public has costs and benefits for the society at large and therefore is not only an expenditure but an investment as well. Thus, the political implications of education surpass the conditions of an individual to be educated, and constitute a strategic set of decisions that affect society at large — hence the importance of education as public policy, and the role of the state.

This dialectical process of forming the individual as a self and as a member of a larger community implies, as a premise in the Western tradition, the need to preserve the treasures of the civilization within the process of socializing the members of each new generation. This becomes even more of an imperative as the nation-state becomes the site, surrounded by borders, in which the pedagogical process is governed.

Organized systems of education operate under the aegis of a nation-state that controls, regulates, coordinates, mandates, finances, and certifies the process of teaching and learning. Not surprisingly, a principal purpose of the educational system so designed is to create a loyal and competent citizen.

The question we are facing now is, To what extent is the educational endeavor affected by processes of globalization that are threatening the autonomy of national educational systems and the sovereignty of the nation-state as the ultimate ruler in democratic societies? At the same time, how is globalization changing the fundamental conditions of an educational system premised on fitting into a community, a community characterized by proximity and familiarity?

The origins, nature, and dynamics of the process of globalization are, therefore, a focus for concern of educational philosophers, sociologists, curriculum workers, teachers, policy makers, politicians, parents, and many others involved with the educational endeavor. The processes of globalization, however defined, seem to have serious consequences for transforming teaching and learning, as they have been understood within the context of educational practices and public policies that are highly national in character.

Many further questions recur in such reflections. How can globalization be defined? Is globalization "real" or merely an ideology? If globalization is an inexorable trend, how does this affect the political economy of countries, and in turn, their culture and education? How are moves toward economic restructuring affecting educational systems worldwide? Is there an international educational organization, and agenda, that could create a new hegemony in curriculum, instruction, and pedagogical practices in general, as well as in policies concerning school financing, research, and evaluation? Are these factors and outcomes symmetrical or homogeneous in their implications for all countries and regions? How does globalization relate to the ongoing process of political struggle in different societies?

In order to capture the gist of social action, we must recognize the *ontological complicity*, as Heidegger and Merleu-Ponty suggested, between the agent (who is neither a subject or a consciousness, nor the mere executant of a role or the carrier of a function) and the social world (which is never a mere "thing" even if it must be constructed as such in the objectivist phase of research). Social reality exists, so to speak, twice, in things and in minds, in fields and in habitus, outside and inside of agents. And when habitus encounters a social world of which it is the product, it finds itself "as a fish in water," it does not feel the weight of the water and takes the world about itself for granted.

The characteristics of globalization that most closely affect education, but these seem to include, at the very least:

— in *economic terms*, a transition from Fordist to Post-Fordist forms of workplace organization; a rise in internationalized advertising and consumption patterns; a reduction in barriers to the free flow of goods, workers, and investments across national borders; and, correspondingly, new pressures on the roles of worker and consumer in society;

— in *political terms*, a certain loss of nation-state sovereignty, or at least the erosion of national autonomy; and, correspondingly, a weakening of the notion of the "citizen" as a unified and unifying concept, a concept that can be characterized by precise roles, rights, obligations, and status;

— in *cultural terms*, a tension between the ways in which globalization brings forth more standardization and cultural homogeneity, while also bringing more fragmentation through the rise of locally oriented movements.

Globalization and State-Education Relationship

In educational terms, there is a growing understanding that the neoliberal version of globalization, particularly as implemented (and ideologically defended) by bilateral, multilateral, and international organizations, is reflected in an educational agenda that privileges, if not directly imposes, particular policies for evaluation, financing, assessment, standards, teacher training, curriculum, instruction, and testing. In the face of such pressures, more study is needed about local responses to defend public education against the introduction of pure market mechanisms to regulate educational exchanges and other policies that seek to reduce state sponsorship and financing and to impose management and efficiency models borrowed from the business sector as a framework for educational decisionmaking. These educational responses are mostly carried out by teacher unions, new social movements, and critical intellectuals, often expressed as opposition to initiatives in education such as vouchers or subsidizing private and parochial schools.

This poses a peculiar problem for analysis. Because the relationships between state and education vary so dramatically according to historical epochs, geographical areas, modes of governance, and forms of political representation, and between the differential demands of varied educational levels (elementary, secondary, higher education, adult, continuing, and nonformal education), any drastic alteration of modes of governance (for instance, the installation of a military dictatorship that may rule for several years before yielding back to democracy), can have multiple, complex, and unpredictable effects on education. This situation calls for a more nuanced historical analysis of the state-education relationship. This problematic is made more difficult by the erosion in the autonomy of the nation-state in all matters, including educational policy matters.

For example, let us consider briefly the situation in Latin America. From the moment in which civil wars were ended, more than a century and a half ago (culminating in the process of national organization in the 1880's), educational systems were created alongside the establishment of borders for countries. The constitution of the nation-states included the creation of strong armies and the promulgation of National Constitutions based on principles drawing from the British Magna Carta, the American Revolution, and the French Revolution, and therefore expressing a strongly liberal underpinning.

Thus, at least three primary state formations predominated in the Latin American experience over the last century and a half. (The exceptions to this trend have been, of course, periods of military intervention, military dictatorship, and revolution, all of which alter the liberal-democratic state form.) These three forms of the state include the *liberal* state promoting liberal education (say, from the 1880s until the crisis of 1929 in some countries, or until around the Second World War in most countries); the *developmentalist* state (around the 1950s until the 1980s), in which there is a consistent pattern of modernization, with a central role played by educational reforms based on the human capital model: and the constitution of different forms of the *neoliberal* state and neoliberal educational policy.

From a historical perspective, this complex connection between education and the state poses a problem for the analysis of the state-education relationship. There is no single way in which these institutions are associated, and so no single way in which they will be affected by the conditions of globalization.

Economically, the pressures of externally imposed austerity conditions (for example, as a condition of IMF loans) may lead to savage reductions in expenditures on education: in other contexts, the desire for increased economic competitiveness and productivity may lead to increased expenditures on education. Politically, some national contexts will organize education around a revitalized conception of nationalism and citizen loyalty (perhaps in reaction to tribal or other fractious loyalties): in other contexts, a notion of cosmopolitan citizenship may prevail, one encouraging travel, foreign language study, and multicultural tolerance.

Culturally, some nations will accept, even encourage, an increased reliance on the media, popular culture, or new communication and information technology, as a window through which to understand one's place in a global world: in other contexts these same trends will give rise to an increase in insularism, suspicion, and resistance to external influences.

Impacts of Global Economic Restructuring

The patterns of global economic restructuring, which emerged in the late seventies, went hand in hand with the implementation of neoliberal policies in many nations. At that time, capitalist management was caught in a profit squeeze, with labor fighting to keep wages high, and foreign competitors pressing them to keep prices down.

As the economy slowed, state revenues failed to keep pace with social expenditures, and taxpayers began to express resentment toward those who benefited the most from state revenues (the state bureaucracy, welfare recipients, institutions receiving state subsidies, and so on.). This led to a breakdown of consensus around the viability and value of the welfare state. The state withdrew from its role as an arbiter between labor and capital, allying itself with capital, and pushing labor into a defensive position.

Economic restructuring reflected a world trend characterized by at least the following elements:

— the globalization of the economy in the context of a new international division of labor and economic integration of national economies (such as emerging common markets and trade agreements);

— the emergence of new exchange relations and arrangements among nations, and among classes and social sectors within each country, and the emergence of new areas, especially in developed countries, where information and services were becoming more important than manufacturing;

— the increasing internationalization of trade, reflected in the increasing capacity to connect markets on an immediate basis and to move capital across national frontiers (currently, 600 major multinational corporations (MNCs) control 25% of the world economy and 80% of world trade);

— the restructuring of the labor market, with the hourly wage being replaced in many settings by piece-work remuneration, and the power of unions undermined by a relaxation or non-enforcement of labor legislation;

— the decrease in capital-labor conflict, mainly due to such factors as the increase of surplus workers (unemployed or underemployed), the intensification of competition and the decrease of profit margins, less protective labor contracts, and the institutionalization of "team concept" strategies;

— the shift from a rigid Fordist model of production to a model based upon increased flexibility in the use of the labor force, inventories, labor processes, and labor markets, and upon the declining costs and increasing speed of moving products and information from one location of the globe to another;

— the rise of new forces of production, with industry shifting from an industrial-mechanical model to one governed by the microchip, robotics, and automatic, self-regulating machines, which in turn has led to the emergence of a high-tech information society based on the computer;

— the growing importance of capital-intensive production, which results in the deskilling or redundancy of large sections of the workforce, a situation that leads to a polarized labor market composed of a small, highly skilled, and well-paid sector on the one hand, and a large, low-skilled, and low-paid sector on the other;

— the increase in the proportion of part-time and female workers, many of them now working out of their homes;

— the increase in the size and importance of the service sector, at the expense of primary and secondary ones; and

— the ever-increasing financial, technological, and cultural gap between more-developed and less-developed countries, with the only exception being the "newly industrialized countries" (NICs).

Economic restructuring also has reflected a deep fiscal crisis and budget reductions affecting the public sector, resulting in the reduction of the welfare state and increased privatization of social services, health, housing, and education. There has been a restructuring of the state/worker relationship in such a way that the social salary (public expenditure distributed in the form of social benefits) diminishes at the expense of individual salaries.

As a result of this, society has been segmented into two sectors: one protected or included by the state, and the other unprotected and excluded. Economic restructuring has led to a model of exclusion that leaves out large sectors of the population, particularly women living in poverty in developed and developing countries.

These elements of economic restructuring have been concomitant with the trend toward globalization. Contrary to Marx and Engels' prediction, the globalization of the economy has produced a unification of capital on a world scale, while workers and other subordinate groups have become more fragmented and divided. In fact, neoliberal restructuring is operating through the impersonal dynamic of capitalist competition in a progressively deregulated common market, enhancing the local impact of global trends. Nation-states have become increasingly internationalized. in the sense that their agencies and policies become adjusted to the rhythms of the new world order.

Economic restructuring has led to an increasing proletarianization and deskilling of jobs. Although high technology is presented as the solution to many economic problems, it has not contributed to raising the standard of living of most people. Even if some jobs are being created in high-tech industries, these jobs are mostly in clerical and assembly work, which pay below-average wages and do not require high skills, or in personal services jobs. Not surprisingly, the most important category of job creation in the United States in the last decade has been in the realm of personal services, including job categories as varied as physical and health trainers to private security services.

Another evident change is that. with the implementation of neoliberal policies, the state has withdrawn from its responsibility to administer public resources to promote social justice. This is being replaced by a blind faith in the market (for example, in calls for increased school privatization, "choice," and vouchers) and the hope that economic growth will generate a spillover to help the poor. or that private charity will pick up what state programs leave out.

Despite calls from the Right to dismantle or reduce the size of the state, skeptical observers of state reduction argue that the main issue is not the state's size. or its expenditures, but the *type* of its interventions and investments. whether promoting welfare and equality on the one hand. or subsidizing corporate growth. through tax incentives or through the rubric of "military spending" on the other.

The neoliberal state, particularly in the more developed societies, and in the developing countries striving to emulate them, is characterized by drastic cutbacks in social spending, rampant environmental destruction, regressive revisions of the tax system, loosened constraints on corporate growth, widespread attacks on organized labor, and increased spending on military "infrastructure."

Corporations are becoming so powerful that many are creating their own postsecondary and vocational education programs. Burger King has opened "Academies" in fourteen U.S. cities, and IBM and Apple are contemplating the idea of opening schools for profit. Whittle Communications (a corporation largely owned by Time Warner and the British Associated Newspapers) not only provides satellite dishes and TV sets in exchange for advertisement to more than 10,000 schools (the "Channel One" project), but is planning to open 1,000 profit-making schools serving two million children within the next ten years.

U.S. corporations are spending upwards of $40 billion each year, approaching the total annual expenditures of all America's four-year and graduate colleges and universities, to train and educate their current employees. Even as early as the mid-eighties, Bell and Howell had 30,000 students in its postsecondary network, and ITT had 25 postsecondary proprietary institutions. It has been reported that AT&T alone performs more education and training functions than any university in the world.

This process of privatizing education is occurring in the context of new relations and arrangements among nations, characterized by a new global division of labor, an economic integration of national economies (common markets, free trade, and so forth), the increasing concentration of power in supranational organizations (such as the World Bank, IMF, UN, EU, and G-7), and what we have called the "internationalization" of nation-states.

The mobility of capital gives capitalists, particularly financial speculators, a great deal of leverage over the nation-state, itself a product of the industrial revolution, and one unequipped in many ways to cope with the basic demands of the postindustrial world. Speculation in national currencies and the self-fulfilling prophecy of international "credit" legitimacy have contributed to an ever-shifting terrain for countries attempting to get their economic houses in order.

Corporate influence over the nation-state is exercised indirectly, through intellectual leadership, instilling in policy makers a new set of values and setting limits on the nation-state's range of options, which is a more effective strategy in changing policy priorities than the explicit threat of punitive sanctions. These new values, aptly reflected in the neoconservative and neoliberal agendas, promote less state intervention and greater reliance on the free market, and more appeal to individual self-interest than to collective rights.

Held claims that "the internationalization of production, finance and other economic resources is unquestionably eroding the capacity of any individual state to control its own economic future...multinational corporations may have a clear national base, but their interest is above all in global profitability. Country of origin is of little consequence for corporate strategy."

Clearly, the growing integration of the economy is pushing toward a borderless world, and provides considerable evidence for the reduced ability of national governments to control their own economies or to define their own national economic aims.

In summary, there are changes at the economic, political, and cultural levels of society that tend to promote and reinforce a more global perspective on social policy.

At an economic level:

— changes in *trade* relations (groups such as GATT, or G-7, that promote the reduction of import taxes, tariffs, and regulations; and the formation of "free trade" regions such as NAFTA or the E.U.);

— changes in *banking and credit* processes (world credit systems such as Visa, ATM's, currency exchange, and capital flow and financial markets that are truly globalized);

— the presence of *international lending agencies* (such as the IMF and World Bank);

— changes in the factors of *production* that have led to the rise of new "Post-Fordist" industries (the knowledge economy, the service sector, tourism, and culture industries);

— the presence of *global corporations* not tied to (or loyal to) any national base or boundary; the *mobility of labor* and the *mobility of companies*, which have thrown labor unions on the defensive; new *technologies* (for the transmission of data, capital, and advertising); and

— new patterns of *consumption* (sometimes termed the "McDonaldization" of taste — fast, standardized, and oriented to convenience over quality), along with new advertising and marketing strategies that promote what George Ritzer calls the "means of consumption".

At the political level, the nation-state survives as a medial institution, far from powerless, but constrained by trying to balance four imperatives:

— responses to transnational capital;

— responses to global political structures (for example, the United Nations) and other nongovernmental organizations;

— responses to domestic pressures and demands, in order to maintain its own political legitimacy; and

— responses to its own internal needs and self-interests.

Most policy initiatives, including educational policies, are formed in the matrix of these four pressures, centered on the nation-state conceived no longer as a sovereign agent, but as an arbiter attempting to balance a range of internal and external pressures and constraints.

Economic factors, such as external debt, the fiscal crisis of the state, or the creation of regional entities such as the European Union are having profound political-economic implications. In this context, the pressures on the nation-state have sharpened a long-standing question of political theory: Is the state a pluralist sphere for the contest of competing interest groups, or is it a non-neutral terrain, reflecting a set of constraints and preoccupations that give special weight to the demands of specific social interests?

It is clear to us that there has been a pronounced shift in the terms of such a question, moving beyond purely statist views of politics to include a focus on new terrains of political contestation, new political actors, such as global social movements, and the constitution of what are, in effect, transnational civil societies.

In cultural terms:

— changes in global media (cable, satellite, CNN, the Internet);

— commercial culture (McDonalds, Nike, the colors of Benneton);

— increased mobility, with vastly enlarged travel and tourism sectors;

— changes in communications technologies;

— worldwide distribution of film, television, and music products;

— an increased presence and visibility of global religions that change local rituals into transnational ones; and

— the global world of sports, both in terms of competitive events (and spectacles) like the Olympics or World Cup, but also, and non-trivially, in terms of sports marketing (apparel, footwear, equipment), sponsorhip/advertising, and global betting and gambling, all show the challenges that confront societies attempting to reconcile their own local and traditional values with the growing globalization of cultures not of their making.

These undeniable changes notwithstanding, however, the effects of globalization are also sometimes exaggerated. Any good observer or world traveler will have noticed that the so-called process of globalization is not so global. Vast segments of the world are almost untouched by many of these globalization dynamics.

What we are seeing is a segmentation (worldwide) between a globalized culture — for instance, the prevalence of an urban, cosmopolitan habitus — and the rest of the world, which sees few of the benefits (to the extent that there are such) of access to the global market or to cosmopolitan cultures. Likewise, as noted previously, the assertion of something called "globalization" is often used to reinforce its "inevitability" and so to suppress attempts to resist it. Many attempts to counteract globalization processes are well in place around the world, as in the fields of ecology and resource management, for example.

Critical Issues

Theoretically, a central dilemma is whether to place the origins of contemporary globalization around 1971-73, with the petroleum crisis that prompted several important technological and economic changes directed toward finding replacement sources for strategic raw materials and searching for new forms of production that would consume less energy and labor.

An important question for many observers is whether we are facing a new historical epoch, the configuration of a new world system, or whether these changes are significant but not unprecedented, paralleled for example by similar changes in the late Middle Ages.

We are in a new historical epoch, a new global order in which the old forms are not dead but the new forms are not yet fully formed. Held has suggested in his *Democracy and Global Order*, for instance, that we are in a new "global Middle Ages," a period reflecting that while the nation-states still have vitality, they cannot control their borders and therefore are subject to all sorts of internal and external pressures.

Furthermore, even if this new global order shows the end of the sovereignty of the nation-state, this situation nevertheless has differential impacts on states according to their position in the world order: states unified in regional alliances, such as NAFTA or the E.U.: emerging or intermediate states, such as Brazil, Korea, India, and China; less developed states, such as Argentina, Hungary, Chile, and South Africa; developing states, including many in Latin America, Asia, and Africa; and underdeveloped states mired in an extreme state of dependency, such as Haiti, some Central American states, Mozambique, Angola, and Albania. Not only is the meaning and impact of "globalization" unsettled, it may operate differently in different parts of the world, and in some contexts have little impact at all. Here, again, globalization is not itself a unified, global phenomenon.

Hence while globalization may reflect a set of very definite technological, economic, and cultural changes, the shape of its significance and its future trends are far from determined. The historical specificity of this process does not necessarily guarantee a symmetrical or homogeneous impact worldwide.

This account of globalization is quite different from the neoliberal account, a discourse about progress and a rising tide that lifts all boats, a discourse that takes advantage of the historical processes of globalization in order to valorize particular economic prescriptions about how to operate the economy — and by implication, prescriptions about how to transform education, politics, and culture.

Certain dualities recur in the literature on this subject. In one widely influential distinction, there are two primary forces at work in the rise of globalization: globalization from above, a process that primarily affects the elites within and across national contexts, and globalization from below, a popular process that primarily draws from the rank-and-file in civil society.

This contrast highlights an important political dynamic (and it makes for a handy, hopeful picture of struggle and resistance on a world scale) but its widespread use obscures the ways in which these two trends are not entirely independent of one another. For example, the groups from "above" and "below" tend to merge in certain nongovernmental organizations; and the popular movements "from below" may still be perceived in certain local contexts as an imposition "from above."

Still other dualities prevail: of tensions between the global and the local; between economic and cultural dimensions of globalization; between globalization viewed as a trend toward homogenization around Western (or, even more narrowly, around American) norms and culture, and globalization viewed as an era of increased contact between diverse cultures, leading to an increase in hybridization and novelty; and between the material and rhetorical effects of globalization — or, as it might be put, between globalization and "globalization." Finally, there is the distinction about whether globalization is a "good thing" or not: Is globalization beneficial to the cause of economic growth, equality, and justice, or is it harmful? Does it promote cultural sharing, tolerance, and a cosmopolitan spirit, or does it yield only the illusion of such understanding, a bland, consumerist appreciation, as in a Disney theme park, which elides issues of conflict, difference, and asymmetries of power?

For us, none of these either/ors captures the subtlety or difficulty of the issues at stake. Each replicates an easy choice between polar alternatives, "good" and "bad" kinds of globalization, rather than a conflicted situation of sustained tensions and difficult choices.

Dilemmas of a Globalized Education System

Is globalization merely deleterious, or are there positive features associated with its practices and dynamics? We have already tried to challenge such an easy frame of judgment. Two features that might be termed "positive" are the globalization of democracy or, at least, a peculiar form of liberal democracy (more a democracy of method than a democracy of content); and the prevalence and expansion of a belief in "human rights" and the growth of organizations attempting to monitor and protect them.

For those fortunate enough to be living in certain sectors of society, globalization is associated with a higher standard of living, not only in the availability of consumer goods, but in occasions for travel and for enriching contact with other world cultures.

The most obvious "evils" of globalization are structural unemployment, the erosion of organized labor as a political and economic force, social exclusion, and an increase in the gap between rich and poor within nations and, especially, worldwide. Some people associate globalization with an increase in urban insecurity due to growing urban violence; with the growing presence of extra-territorial, extra-state movements that thwart international development and may pose serious threats to security, peace, stability, and development (such as drug trafficking, mafias, merchants of weapons of mass destruction, or terrorist organizations).

But is it possible to sort out the benefits from the evils? Indeed, are "benefits" from one standpoint "evils" from the standpoint of others? In one sense, the framework of such judgments needs to be not simply a matter of whether globalization is "really happening" or not, but of globalization *in what respects* and *on whose terms*?

A number of developing countries, such as China or Malaysia, have become increasingly suspicious of globalization and have tried to find ways to constrain its effects on their national way of life. Yet, at the same time they desire some of the benefits of participation in a global economy and exchange of goods and information. A major question today is the extent to which societies will be able to pick and choose the ways in which, and the degree to which, they can participate in a global world; or whether, as with other Faustian bargains, there is no halfway alternative.

Similarly, both below and beyond the national level, there are clearly regional and traditional movements for whom globalization is something to be resisted vigorously. The rise of some new social movements and the role of local and international nongovernmental organizations exert an influence that may be termed "counterglobalization."

In some instances these groups are equally "global" in character (international human rights organizations, such as Amnesty International; environmental organizations, such as Greenpeace; or labor organizations such as the ILO). In other cases they are anti-globalization, profoundly resistant to the economic, political, and cultural interpenetration of different societies and cultures. While globalization is clearly happening, its form and shape are being determined by patterns of resistance, some with more progressive intentions than others.

Is it possible, then, to give general answers to the question of how globalization is affecting educational policy and practice worldwide? There can be no single answer; national and local economic, political, and cultural changes are affected by, and actively responding to, globalizing trends within a broad range of patterns. Indeed, because education is one of the central arenas in which these adaptations and responses occur, it will be one of the most myriad of institutional contexts. Hence, the answers developed will require a careful analysis of trends in education, including:

— the currently popular policy "buzz words" (privatization, choice, and decentralization of educational systems) that drive policy formation in education and prevailing research agendas based in rational organization and management theories;

— the role of national and international organizations in education, including teacher unions, parent organizations, and social movements ;

— the new scholarship on race, class, gender, and the state in education (and hence concerns about multiculturalism and the question of identity in education, critical race theory, feminism, postcolonialism, diasporic communities, and new social movements.

Questions about the role of participatory action research, popular education, and multicultural democratic struggle emerge as central in these debates. From these critical perspectives might emerge new educational models to confront the winds of change, including education in the context of new popular cultures and nontraditional social movements (and hence the role of cultural studies to understand them); new models of rural education for marginalized areas and the education of the poor; new models for migrant education, for the education of street children, for the education of girls and women in general, but particularly in the context of traditional societies and cultures that have suppressed women's educational aspirations; new models of partnerships for education (between state, NGO, third sector, and in some instances religious or private organizations); new models for adult literacy and nonformal education; new models of university/business relationships; and new models for educational financing and school organization (for instance, charter schools).

Some reform initiatives have been actively supported by UNESCO and other UN agencies. These include, for instance, reforms toward universal literacy and universal access to education; educational quality as a key component of equity; education as lifelong education; education as a human right; education for peace, tolerance, and democracy; eco-pedagogy, or how education can contribute to sustainable ecological development (and hence to an eco-economy); and educational access and new technologies of information and communication. Thus, the influence of globalization upon educational policies and practices can be seen to have multiple, and conflicting, effects. Not all of these can be classified simply as beneficial or not, and some are being shaped by active tensions and struggles.

At the economic level, because globalization is affecting employment it touches upon one of the primary traditional goals of education, preparation for work. Schools will need to reconsider this mission in light of changing job markets in a Post-Fordist work environment; new skills and the flexibility to adapt to changing job demands and, for that matter, changing jobs over a lifetime; and dealing with an increasingly competitive international labor pool.

Yet, schools are not only concerned with preparing students as producers; increasingly, schools help shape consumer attitudes and practices as well, as encouraged by the corporate sponsorship of educational institutions and of products, both curricular and extracurricular, that confront students every day in their classrooms. This increasing commercialization of the school environment has become remarkably bold and explicit in its intentions.

The broader economic effects of globalization tend to force national educational policies into a neoliberal framework that emphasizes lower taxes; shrinking the state sector and "doing more with less"; promoting market approaches to school choice (particularly vouchers); rational management of school organizations; performance assessment (testing); and deregulation in order to encourage new providers (including online providers) of educational services.

At the political level, a repeated point here has been the constraint on national/state policy making posed by external demands from transnational institutions. Yet, at the same time that economic coordination and exchange have become increasingly well-regulated, and as stronger institutions emerge to regulate global economic activity, with globalization there has also been a growing internationalization of global conflict, crime, terrorism, and environmental issues. but with an inadequate development of political institutions to address them.

Here, again, educational institutions may have a crucial role to play in addressing these problems, and the complex network of intended and unintended human consequences that have followed from the growth of global corporations, global mobility, global communication, and global expansion. In part, this awareness may help to foster a more critical conception of what education for "world citizenship" requires.

Global changes in culture deeply affect educational policies, practices, and institutions. Particularly in advanced industrial societies, for instance, the question of "multiculturalism" takes on a special meaning in a global context. How does the discourse of liberal pluralism, which has been the dominant framework for multicultural education in developed societies — to learn about different others as a way of living with them and coordinating social activity with them within a compact of mutual tolerance and respect — extend to a global order in which the gulf of differences becomes wider, the sense of interdependence and common interest more attenuated, and the grounding of affiliation more abstract and indirect (if it exists at all)? With the growing global pressures on local cultures, is it education's job to help preserve them? How should education prepare students to deal with the terms of local, regional, national, and transnational conflict, as cultures and traditions whose histories of antagonism may have been held partly in suspension by strong, overarching nation-states break loose as those institutions lose some of their power and legitimacy? To the degree that education can help support the evolving construction of the self and, at a more general level, the constitution of identities, how can multiculturalism as a social movement, as citizenship education, and as an antiracist philosophy in curriculum intervene in the dynamics of social conflict emerging between global transformations and local responses?

In this context, for example, current debates over bilingualism in the United States are surprisingly limited both in their theoretical content and their political foresight. From a theoretical perspective, it really makes no sense to argue *against* the teaching and learning of multiple languages: if anything, students need to develop even more proficiency than just bilingualism. The European experience with youth who are proficient in several languages finds that such skills facilitate interpersonal, academic, and social communication, expand intellectual horizons, and encourage appreciation and tolerance for different cultures.

In this and other respects, the global context presents a fundamentally different sort of challenge to education than in the Enlightenment framework. Whereas previously education was more focused on the needs and development of the individual, with an eye toward helping the person fit into a community defined by relative proximity, homogeneity, and familiarity, education for life in a global world broadens the outlines of "community" beyond the family, the region, or the nation.

Today the communities of potential affiliation are multiple, dislocated, provisional, and ever-changing. Family, work, and citizenship, the main sources of identification in Enlightenment education, remain important, certainly, but are becoming more ephemeral, compromised by mobility (whether voluntary or diasporic) and competition with other sources of affiliation, including the full range of what can be termed, in Benedict Anderson's phrase, "imagined communities."

Whereas schools or (before that) tutors acted *in loco parentis*, preparing learners for a relatively predictable range of future opportunities and challenges, schools today confront a series of conflicting, and changing, ad hoc expectations, directed to unpredictable alternative paths of development and to constantly shifting reference points of identification. As a result, educational aims that have more to do with flexibility and adaptability (for instance, in responding to rapidly changing work demands and opportunities), with learning how to coexist with others in diverse (and hence often conflict-riven) public spaces, and with helping to form and support a sense of identity that can remain viable within multiple contexts of affiliation, all emerge as new imperatives.

How such new educational imperatives get worked out in particular national and cultural settings depends upon two overarching sets of issues. The first is whether, given the decreasing role and influence of the nation-state in unilaterally determining domestic policies, and given the fiscal crisis of public revenues in most societies, there will be a corresponding decline in the state's commitment to educational opportunity and equality, or whether there will simply be a greater turn toward the market, privatization, and choice models that regard the public as consumers who will only obtain the education they can afford. More broadly, will these changes produce an overall decline in the civic commitment to public education itself?

The second key issue is whether the troubles that educational systems experience today, which are not all related to the processes of globalization, signal a more deeply felt and decisive dilemma in developed and developing societies: the question of governability in the face of increasing diversity (and an increased awareness of diversity); permeable borders and an explosion in worldwide mobility; and media and technology that create wholly new conditions shaping affiliation and identification. What is the role of education in helping to shape the attitudes, values, and understandings of a multicultural democratic citizen who can be part of this increasingly cosmopolitan world?

At least some of the manifestations of globalization as a historical process are here to stay. Even if the particular form of "globalization" presented by the neoliberal account can be regarded as an ideology that serves to justify policies serving particular interests but not others. the fact is that part of this account is based in real changes.

2

Technological Impacts on Education

The exponential expansion in new information and communication technologies is one result of the general process towards digitisation . What is emerging is the capacity for the convergence of telecommunications, computer and audio-visual technologies 'previously separated by techniques, legislation and modes of distribution'. The convergence between previously distinct forms of communication has organizational and technical consequences. At the functional level, the once distinct communication media – radio broadcasting, telecommunications and computer technology sectors – have the potential to offer a more hybrid range of services. At the technical level, old distinctions within the transmission infrastructure could become obsolete. Where information is processed in digital form, distribution systems then become multi-purpose.

The use of new information and communication technologies, and especially of the Internet, has expanded dramatically within the decade. Increasingly, as new technologies are becoming integrated into educational settings.

there are new learning opportunities for learners and intermediaries (teachers, health and agricultural extension workers); there is the potential for communicating across geographical distances and time differences with ease, for accessing new pools of information and resources, and for participating in new learning networks and partnerships.In communications, as in every other sector, these developments have been unbalanced. 'Overshadowing the utilization of the new information and communication technologies in education are worldwide disparities in access to these technologies'.

Most developing countries lack the basic infrastructure and training needed for gaining access. This 'digital divide' compounds existing inequalities between people within and between countries; the disparities in access are not random but correlate strongly with income, education, ethnic origin, location and gender. Learners from developing countries therefore face additional risks: the concentration of the ownership of communications systems; the dominance of western educational models and market leaders; and exposure to what may be seen as new forms of political, cultural and linguistic colonialism. The English language dominates. It accounts for 85-90 per cent of Internet messages, 80 per cent of websites and 80-85 per cent of all scientific and technical information in abstracted, published or computer-stored form.

The consequences may be to downgrade other languages. But, at the same time, the use of English, already the key international language, means that those with some capacity in it have their access to learning widened by the new technologies. The development of the Internet therefore poses difficult ethical challenges. These may bear particularly on aid agencies. There is a danger that funding to support Internet development may only nurture an illusion of egalitarianism while differences in access to computer communication in fact shore up existing inequalities. Agency investment in this sector has also been criticized as principally helping the communications industry penetrate new markets and set up new dependencies. Aid for Internet development might divert funds from more traditional forms of development; the balance between funding for books and teachers and funding for technology is not easy. At the same time there is an obvious downside to decisions against funding Internet growth.

One response to the demand for investment in communications technology for education has been the pooling of resources between bilateral and multilateral aid agencies in the form of large-scale, collaborative and sectorwide, capacity-building and training initiatives in telecommunications. Examples include the InfoDev programme (World Bank), the International Programme for the Development of Communications (UNESCO), the Intergovernmental Informatics Programme (UNESCO), BellaNet (CIDA, IDRC and UNDP) and the Telecentre Fund (ITU, UNESCO and IDRC). Emphasis has also been placed on innovative ways to develop rural communications, including the notion of developing public access points and resource centres such as community access centres, multi-purpose rural tele-centres and public communications booths.

The ground statistics, however, remain salutary: in Africa as a whole, radio covers 75 per cent of the population, television 40 per cent and the Internet 0.1 per cent. Some

62 per cent of all telephones lines in the entire world are installed in just 23 countries, one-quarter of all countries in the world have less than one telephone per 100 people, 84 per cent of mobile phone subscribers, 91 per cent of fax machines and 97 per cent of Internet host computers are in industrialized countries; 63 per cent of users are male and 37 per cent are female, a ratio that has remained consistent over several years.

The 1990s seen the end of some state monopolies of media, a rise in commercial media, and a growth in satellite and community broadcasting. These changes have ushered in an increasingly fragmented media environment and, in some countries, regulatory and legislative bodies more favourable to pluralism. All these developments have influenced the use of communications technology for basic education. One development is that, in some developing countries, there have been new opportunities for commercial and small community radio stations to develop educational programming. For example, in some countries of French-speaking West Africa – Benin, Burkina Faso, Guinea, Mali and Senegal – the move away from an exclusively urban-concentrated, government monopoly has resulted in a new wave of community radio programmes for non-formal and adult education, targeted to particular communities and often in a range of African languages.

Another development is that audio and video technologies have become cheaper, smaller, more reliable and easier to use. This has made them usable in a wide variety of contexts and by a broader, less professional range of people. The media have thus become more accessible to more organizations and individuals working in basic education. Part of this trend can also be seen in the emerging and innovative private sector in rural communication – video rental shops, video recording services for weddings, photocopying, local and long distance telephone shops, fax services, photo-taking, film processing, newspaper and magazine kiosks, book-stores and pre-recorded audio-cassette outlets. One downside of the privatization process is that many educational bodies that once had free access to satellites or airtime on national government stations no longer do so.

Since the Jomtien conference, most energy and most attention has been given to the expansion of schooling through government action. But this is not the whole story; non-governmental organizations in particular have played a number of roles in the expansion of education and in rethinking approaches to expansion and change. Although it is difficult to quantify, it seems likely that non-governmental organizations have increased their involvement in basic education, alongside governments.Their work has benefited from their inherent advantages: modest scale, an ability to respond quickly to emergency situations; local knowledge and continuous presence in particular regions. All these have enabled them to make small-scale interventions and target specific, often excluded, populations such women farmers. One consequence of this is a new pattern of co-operation between government agencies and non-governmental organisations in basic education.

Many non-governmental organizations have brought to their work, and to these cooperative developments, a commitment to a participatory style of working, arguing that: Self-determination is an important characteristic of development. People's participation in their own empowerment is critical to foster a sense of dignity and self-reliance. Small and short-term projects may work better than long-term and big projects. Also projects that begin small and then expand carefully have better chances of success. This emphasis on the participation of rural and urban communities in decision-making has led to a proliferation of grass-roots initiatives, and community-based and non-formal education programmes, and has influenced the choice and use of technologies within them.

Participatory approaches fit more easily with small-scale, locally developed projects than with those that are centrally planned and rely on broadcasting on a large scale. There is, therefore, a tension between the demand for a participatory approach and attempts to use mass media on the large scale which their technology allows and from which their economic benefits flow. While much non-governmental organization attention has gone to general programmes of basic education, many have also given particular attention to the needs of marginalized basic education groups – girls in some societies, special needs, war children, displaced communities, travellers, street children, adolescents, remote, excluded, religious and ethnic communities. Here, too, in contexts where conventional approaches to basic education have been least successful, the more imaginative projects have benefited from non-govern-mental organizations' freedom of activity and commitment to participatory methodologies. Mainstream status of open and distance learning.

During the 1990s, open and distance learning moved firmly away from its status as the poor relation and began to be regarded as a legitimate part of mainstream education to be used separately or in combination with face-to-face education. There are now closer links, at all levels, between conventional education and open and distance learning. Another drive towards legitimacy has been the professionalization of open and distance learning – the proliferation of specialist international, regional, and national agencies, organizations, interest groups, professional journals and conferences.

The last forty years have seen a steady exponential reduction in the cost of manufacturing both computer memory and computer processors. This has now resulted in the availability of powerful 'personal' computers linked by networks to 'server' computers holding data and programs associated with different enterprises. A key aspect of the contemporary personal computer is the graphical user interface which makes it possible for the user to control many aspects of the computer's functions by pointing at pictures rather than by typing instructions.

The educational institutions of some countries are relatively computer rich and some schools now have a computer in every classroom, or classrooms in which for a number of hours a week pupils may have individual use of a networked personal computer. In other countries pupils or even teachers will not encounter computers as part of routine schooling. Both between countries and within countries access to computer technology is very heterogeneous, but the long-term tendency will continue to be greater access to powerful computers designed for individual use. For educationalists it is important to recognise that modern computers with their keyboards, small screen and pointing devices such as mice have evolved into personal media which for the user are similar to books and notepads and quite different from blackboards and lectures. At the same time it is becoming easier to work with others via personal computers, because the additional technological push associated with this decade is the increasing integration of computer and communication technologies. This integration manifests itself in various ways with a key historical distinction between asynchronous modes and synchronous modes of learning and working.

Asynchronous modes include electronic mail, computer conferencing, access to remote databases and to the World Wide Web. In these modes the provider of information knows that there is an audience for which they are preparing information. This may be an individual learner, a class or anyone with interest and Internet access who will read and perhaps react to the information provided at some unspecified future time. Synchronous modes include digital broadcasting, screen sharing, on-line blackboards, video links and audio links. In these modes, the learners and teachers can respond to each other in real time, selecting and storing information for future use or making changes to a running computer simulation whose consequences are immediately apparent to the other active learners and teachers. We can predict an integration of tools used by learners for sending messages and sharing running simulations with the tools for authoring materials and for browsing databases and World Wide Web pages. Such integration is highly desirable for ease of use and without it there is a real risk that the proliferation of new digital information sources will create an unmanageable burden for teachers and learners.

The three critical aspects are the integration of information and communication technologies, the integration of synchronous and asynchronous modes of use and the integration of tools for search and construction of digital learning materials. Such integration could make networks much more transparent and the Internet as easy to use as the telephone, especially as computer input devices become even simpler and support pointing and speech rather than requiring the typing of strings of colons. dots and slashes.

The educational systems around the world are subject to resource pressures of varying degree and in many parts of the world there is limited access to physical networks that can support reliable high speed digital communication. So the cost of the technology is critical. We can now predict with some confidence the eventual possibility of small robust wireless networked personal computers that are relatively cheap to manufacture and that have the additional functionality of a telephone, television. fax. etc. But the way the ubiquitous computer of the future will be marketed is much harder to predict. Given the past behaviour of the leading companies and the fact that there can be commercial benefits associated with incompatible hardware. software and communication standards it is necessary to be very cautious about the timing of universal world educational access to the technologies that are needed to support virtual learning environments.

Educational Technologies

In the past decade, digital technologies have transformed the way deducation is accomplished, as well as affecting its potential impact on markets for copyrighted works. The relevant technologies can be broken down into three major categories:

— technologies that facilitate licensing:

— technologies that deliver the content of the course: and

— technologies that protect the delivered content.

Within the last category, a further distinction can be made between technologies that restrict access, and technologies that restrict or detect uses of works after access has been gained. One area of technology that facilitates licensing is the ability to attach licensing-related information to a work in a digital format. This information can be linked to or embedded in the work, and accessed by the user. In some instances the user will need special software to read information imperceptibly embedded in the work, and in others he can click on an external link to the information. Information so accessed can identify the copyright owner, point the user to the appropriate licensing site, or list licensing terms and conditions.Also useful are online rights and permissions services that can support a range of license and delivery functions, although not all services offer all functions.

Electronic licensing and electronic delivery are separable, independent activities, and either or both can be accomplished by the same online service. Such services can provide central access to a large group of materials, standardized licensing terms that can be customized according to the content provider, and a quick turn-around time for requests. Several different online rights and permissions services are currently in use or development.

The online permissions process itself allows a high degree of specialization. Menus for these online requests can divide users into different categories and subject them to different licensing terms, including grants of permission without a fee. For example, an educational requester could be asked to specify whether the proposed use is for a classroom. seminar, or dissertation. Users could be asked to identify themselves as nonprofit or for-profit. accredited or non-accredited, or any other characteristics that are significant to the copyright owner. The user could also respond to standard queries on the method of delivery. the size of the class. or the security of the website.

Any information relevant to the decision whether to license and how much to charge can be obtained. and this information can be used to generate an automatic response based on pre-established agreements between the service and the copyright owner, or to query the copyright owner directly for permission. In addition to processing licensing requests. some services may also accept payment for the license and deliver the content to the user digitally. Depending on the particular service, the material could be delivered with whatever technological protections the copyright owner specifies already attached.

As well as enabling licensing and delivery to take place online, technology can also facilitate access to licensors by the direct linking of works in a digital form to rights and permissions databases. This may be done with a link. such as an icon, at the end of text or an image. that a user may click on to go straight to an online licensing database. An important development in licensing for digital uses is the convergence of permissions systems with other systems designed to identify and protect material. In the analog world. licensing tends to be a discrete transaction. separate from how the user gains. Access to the material or what the user is able to do with the material once she has it. In the digital world, these functions are converging. A single online site may authorize use of a work, accept payment for that use. deliver a copy of the work to the user. and attach technological protections.

Distance education today is delivered via both analog and digital technologies, including diverse combinations of telephone connections, telecourses, video conferences and computer transmissions. Because our mandate is to consider issues relating to the use of digital technologies. particularly the need for an exemption "for distance education through digital networks," we focus here on the use of digital network technology. Other types of digital technologies may also be used to deliver distance education, such as digital television broadcasts or videoconferencing. These are examples of traditional media being used to carry digital. instead of analog. information.

Telecourses and video conferences incorporate different degrees of interactivity, and may involve one-way video with two-way audio, or two-way video and two-way audio. At the highest level of interactivity, videoconferencing allows instructors and students to see and speak to each other in real time as if they were in a classroom together. These types of digital technologies function much like their analog counterparts, but are usually capable of carrying more information more efficiently. It is important to note that even non-networked transmissions, whether digital or analog, may incorporate elements of digital network technology. For example, telecourses or video conferences are often transmitted in conjunction with a computer connection between the students and the instructor, allowing simultaneous online interaction.

The computer is the most versatile of distance education instruments, since it can incorporate or perform the same function as a television or telephone, as well as providing more interactivity, delivering more content, and supporting more comprehensive services than any other single medium. Computers can be used to transmit texts and graphics, connect users in a variety of real-time and asynchronous dialogues, deliver messages between users, and receive both audio and video transmissions.

There are several commercial software products available to help educators construct online courses for students to access through personal computers. These products are basically a template of a blank course website, offering a choice of many of the technologies common to such courses. The instructor is then free to fill in the site with content, and to choose which of the available options she wants to incorporate.

Despite the use of these common templates, there is no "typical" online distance education course. When the concept of a class is transported to a virtual context, it is no longer constrained by the attributes of a physical classroom, such as the duration of a lesson, the ways in which materials can be used in class, and the schedule of the teacher and students.

The virtual classroom can be defined by its ability to be tailored to the needs of different instructors, students and subject matters. The commercial templates are designed to be customized by each instructor. In addition, many instructors, or the information services of their institutions, build their own courses from scratch.

Factors such as the technological sophistication of the target student body, and the level of technology available to these students, will influence how many of the available "bells and whistles" are used in a given course. There are constantly new products produced for this market. and numerous tools that can be employed in an online course.

Role of Computers

Computers have been used in an attempt to change. strengthen and improve basic education in a variety of different ways and for a variety of different purposes. We start by looking at the rationales for using computers in education and then at strategies for making them available to learners. It is worth distinguishing between various different rationales for using computers in education so that policy decisions can sensibly reflect educational purpose. An analysis by the Commonwealth Secretariat. which drew on reviews of Commonwealth- wide practice. usefully distinguished four rationales for introducing computers to education: the development of Internet communications means that we now need to add a fifth.

Rationale 1: To build a resource of people who are highly skilled in the use of information technology. Where governments see information technology as a means of strengthening the economy, and want to develop a workforce with vocational skills for computer-related activities. computer-education programmes have been set up to develop a cadre of people with specialist skills.

Rationale 2: To equip all students for a future in which technological awareness and basic computer skills will increasingly be important for greater numbers of citizens. Countries have adopted this approach as they see that. whether or not the country is likely to be a producer of computer hardware or software, their citizens need to be in a strong position to take advantage of technological developments as they arise.

Rationale 3: To use the technology to enhance the existing curriculum and to improve the way in which it is developed. Computer-assisted learning programs, in which the computer takes over some of the activity of the teacher, fall within this rationale.

Rationale 4: To promote change in education by moving towards a more relevant curriculum and a new definition of the teacher's role. Some computer projects have been designed to shift the curriculum in the direction of practical learning of information-handling and communication skills rather than concentration on memory.

Rationale 5: To allow learners to seek information from databases, especially through the Internet, and use computer technology to communicate with other schools, colleges and learning communities. This rationale opens up new learner-initiated opportunities. This fifth rationale has been developed in the last five years.

Of course the rationales overlap and national policies may embrace more than one but their curricular and cost implications are different. The first rationale leads to investment in courses at the upper end of secondary education, in vocational training and in tertiary education. Whole-hearted adoption of the second rationale, concerning the education of all future citizens, suggests that computer-related education should be at the upper end of the universal stage of education. It is likely, too, that educational content will rely on generic software – allowing children to develop basic skills in wordprocessing or the use of databases and spreadsheets for example – rather than the use of subject-specific computer-aided learning. The third rationale has been the subject of the most severe criticism; early computer-aided learning proved to have high unit costs and, in many cases, simply offered an expensive way of offering drill and practice, with keyboard and mouse instead of pen and paper. The fourth and fifth rationales both suggest that, if computers are to be used in school, it is necessary to think through their consequences for the curriculum; changes in the curriculum will not occur through technology alone.

The fifth rationale presents new opportunities for reshaping the curriculum but demands not only that schools should have access to computers, but also have, and can pay for, access to the Internet. No matter which rationale dominates, the use of computers in the classroom presents significant demands to ministries of education. Computer equipment – hardware – needs to be provided and accompanied by appropriate software. Staff using computers need training. Where computers are used mainly, or even partly, for access to the Internet, then reliable telephone access and an agreement with an Internet service provider are also required. We look at the costs involved below and turn next to the strategic issues involved in getting access to computer technologies for schools, and in some cases for getting access to the Internet.

At present, few low-or middle-income countries have been able to develop nationwide programmes for the use of computers in the classroom. Where there are programmes to develop educational capacity in information and communication technology, they tend either to concentrate on tertiary education or to be limited to a small number of.

usually, urban, schools in a pilot project. These initiatives may form the first stages in an overall government strategy or be piecemeal developments dictated by budgetary limitations, political interest and serendipity.

Throughout the world, there is a clear pecking order when integrating communication technologies into the formal educational system – tertiary downwards and with primary education low on the list. This situation is changing mainly in Organisation for Economic Co-operation and Development (OECD) countries and newly industrialized countries (NIC) for various reasons: national communications policies; increased governmental funding; the integration of the technologies into all levels of national curricula; generally far cheaper hardware and software and increased private ownership. These governments are now funding nationwide initiatives to build up hardware, software and accompanying skills at all educational levels, including the lower secondary, primary and even nursery levels. As a result, various different approaches have been adopted to enable schools to get access to computer hardware and software. Five approaches can be identified:

1. direct provision of computer hardware and software to existing schools,
2. building new customised schools or computer suite annexes,
3. bringing resources to schools via mobile units,
4. providing access for children via a variety of community-based resource centres, e.g. libraries, technology access community centres, non-profit organizations, and

5. mediated access – where someone with access to a computer and Internet helps children who do not.

The first three strategies bring computers to individual primary schools. The fourth takes children out of school to computers off-site. In the fifth, the child does not have actual hands-on access to computers but benefits, directly or indirectly, from someone who does. Strategies 1 and 2 put computers into individual primary schools enabling pupils to have permanent and regular access to them. But heavy demands accompany computer supply. In some cases, mainly in industrialized countries and where it is difficult to adapt existing buildings, strategy two has been favoured with the building of new annexes within schools. Where it is not possible to equip every school, Strategy 3 involves the development of mobile units equipped with satellite and computer equipment. Units can then visit schools on a regular basis, thus offering limited access to a number of schools within a whole region and on regular basis. They are also a means for bringing technology to marginalized learners such as girls in segregated schools and unemployed youth with no access to formal schooling. Strategy 4 involves making use of computers somewhere out-side the school. A number of countries have developed telecentres, or public access points to computer facilities. These have parallels to the 'early days of telephones. In those days, only the elite had their own telephones, so society evolved the concept of public telephones, which anyone could use, paying only the cost of their actual use' . Similarly, telecentres are public places where people can come to use computers. Telecentres exist in a diversity of forms.

Some are commercial while others are not-for-profit: some are free, while others charge. They can operate on an appointment or drop-in basis. Some offer training in software applications and provide induction to new users while others operate on a solely self-access basis for experienced users (wanting e-mail, on-line distance-education courses, Internet access and computer games). Some are highly equipped, staffed telecentres offering a wide range of other technological facilities such as reprographics, television/video, fax, telephones. Others are unstaffed kiosks. In some, the telecentre is part of a wider community education centre catering for different target groups, including school children, and offering classes and meeting rooms. Telecentres exist in range of locations including libraries, bus stops, cafés, shopping malls and voluntary sector premises. Strategy 5 provides more restricted access to computer facilities. It assumes that, even without direct access, the schoolchild can benefit, directly or indirectly, from someone or some institution that does have access to information and communication resources and, in particular, access to the Internet. This type of strategy is a new development, set to expand, and we are beginning to see innovative initiatives, large and small.Strategies 3, 4 and 5 hold particular significance to developing countries for overcoming access problems created by economic, infrastructural and geographical challenges.

The pooling of resources, through community networks, resource centres, and telecentres has been seen as an important way forward and an 'eminently sensible social and political approach' providing the road to wider and more equitable technological access. In high-income countries, the first four strategies commonly operate at primary and junior secondary levels. Provision of computers to individual schools is widespread and it is increasingly the norm to find upwards of one computer per classroom in state primary schools. At the top end, we can see primary schools with classroom computers as well as dedicated computer suites with one computer per two children. Strategies 3 and 4 are often an extension of well-established regional library service systems. Increasingly, well-supported national library services have expanded from books to include the lending of commercial or educational CD-ROMs and video- and audiocassettes. In addition to computerized self-access centres for adults, many libraries have a dedicated children's section with computers and software, to be used on a school visit, as an after-school club and on a drop-in basis. Many children also benefit from privately owned computers to which they have access at home. In combination these strategies create a range of educational opportunities for school children.

These initiatives are led by an increasingly wide number of drivers often working in collaboration – governments, multi- and bilateral donor agencies, non-governmental organizations, trusts, the communications industry, companies via tax benefits, computer recycling and donation schemes. Most of the initiatives, particularly the high-tech ones, are in a pilot stage, especially among least developed countries, and have, understandably, tended to prioritize learning opportunities for teachers, extension workers and people operating small businesses rather than for young learners.

Alongside acclaim for the educational strengths of information and communication technology there is a widespread concern that access to it tends to entrench existing inequalities not only between but within countries. Within low- and middle-income developing countries, for example, a very clear divide in access to computers exists between private and public schools, urban and rural areas. Similar disparities are reported from OECD and NIC countries despite the much higher level of resources they can devote to the technologies.

Role of Broadcasting Media

Both radio and television have long been used in education, to raise the quality of education within school and to extend teaching to audiences outside. Work of this kind continues. Many countries, of all income categories, continue to offer schools' broadcasts. Radio is widely used for public and adult education, often as an auxiliary to the work of other extension agencies. Developments in broadcasting have been influenced by the social and technological changes identified above. The shift of emphasis away from public-service broadcasting to a deregulated sector, increasingly dominated by small stations and transmitters, has been accompanied by technical changes. Many of the newer stations are broadcasting in FM only; the move away from medium-wave, AM, frequencies are reducing national coverage. It is possible that direct satellite broadcasting may, again, bring extremely wide broadcast coverage.

At present, however, direct broadcasting by satellite exists on a trial basis only, and requires relatively expensive and specialist receivers. With these caveats, radio and television broadcasting remain an important means for supporting existing formal education. Three approaches have been followed in using broadcasting to support basic education:

— direct class teaching which substitutes for teachers on a temporary basis;

— school broadcasting and

— general children's programming on mainstream national and commercial radio and television stations.

One variant of the first approach – interactive radio instruction – has attracted much international interest, and is discussed below. It is distinguished by three main features. It is designed for direct teaching, rather than enrichment; broadcasts demand frequent responses by children as they listen; projects have generally devoted significant energies and investment in curriculum development so that their development costs have been higher than those of conventional radio.

Direct class teaching which substitutes for teachers on a temporary basis: The first approach has been dominated by a series of Interactive Radio Instruction (IRI) projects. These bring ready-made 20–30 minute direct teaching and learning exercises to the classroom on a daily basis. The radio lessons, developed around specific learning objectives at particular levels of maths, science, health and languages in national curricula, are intended to improve the quality of classroom teaching and to act as a regular, structured aid to poorly trained classroom teachers in under-resourced schools.

Children interact with the radio presenter by answering questions, singing or performing practical tasks in carefully timed pauses in the audio script. Teachers can prepare or integrate the lesson in their own way or where available, according to suggested extension activities in printed teachers' notes. Successive evaluations have demonstrated the educational effectiveness of IRI: the children consistently perform as well as or better than control groups in tests; it can narrow gaps in achievement between rural and urban children and between boys and girls; where teaching quality is low, it promotes greater standardization of teaching in schools; the methods and models in the programmes can contribute to a teacher's professional development.

School broadcasting: The second approach is school broadcasting. Unlike IRI, school broadcasting is not intended to bear the main burden of direct classroom instruction. Instead, the aim is to provide teachers and learners with complementary resources and learning experiences not locally available. Teachers can choose to slot them into their class work. These programmes, geared to national curricula, are available in a range of subjects and often with back-up resources (print, cassettes or CD-ROMs). Typical strategies include storytelling, dramatizations and interviews. They can be used according to broadcasting schedules or, where technology permits, the teacher can get them recorded for later use at more convenient times. In the latter case, broadcasting stations are used to disseminate educational materials.

Schools' broadcasting materials give greater control to the teachers than IRI, particularly when in cassette form, and help teachers draw on a wider range of resources and use a multi-media, multi-channel teaching approach. However, it is a strategy that depends very strongly on the ability of the teacher to integrate the materials into their classroom. The lesson here, as with IRI, is that educational broadcasting cannot afford to skimp on teacher and producer training. We can see radio and television schools broadcasting in a range of countries and in a variety of organizational patterns.

Some, in high-income countries, are based within large broadcasting corporations, have extensive programming and can broadcast over several national radio and television channels, sometimes on dedicated educational channels. Others are units based within the Ministry of Education, and part of collaboration between the Ministry of Information (where the broadcasters are located), Curriculum Development Centres and a book production and materials resources unit.

The latter is typical of lower-income developing countries. They tend to have a far smaller output that is restricted to certain slots within national or local broad-casting schedules. Regional or community radio stations can often reach only modest numbers of schools but may be able to extend their influence if they can supply programmes in cassette form or arrange to share material with other radio stations. Within industrialized countries, school broadcasters can expect schools to be equipped with recording facilities and therefore freer of broadcasting schedules than in poorer countries where recording equipment cannot be assumed.

Non-formal children's programming: The third approach – non-formal children's programming – consists of radio and television programmes on community, national and international stations aimed at children in or out of school at the primary and junior secondary level. These may provide general and informal educational opportunities and exist in a variety of radio and television forms, including popular culture quizzes, story-telling and educational cartoons. Mainstream children's programming has been gaining increasing attention in the shift towards sophisticated, intergenerational and multi-channel communication strategies and growing recognition as an undervalued educational resource. An emphasis on the need for links between formal and non-formal education, the recognition that learning is an intergenerational phenomenon and that children play a crucial role in teaching each other have all led to an increased concern with informal and non-formal opportunities for learning both in and out of school. Mainstream children's programming has a role to play here. We can see this development most clearly in recent types of health campaigning which are no longer conceived as one-off projects but highly planned long-term campaigns based on extensive formative research. Generally, these combine popular, prime-time radio and television programmes with a wide range of supporting activities directed towards different target groups the community. Increasingly schools are taken into account in these campaigns.

One major stumbling block here is that children's programming is particularly vulnerable where market forces rule: advertisers, marketers and managers see less profit in children's programming than for other target groups; children's programming is neither an easy nor a cheap option compared to other programming. Where it does exist, rampant commercialism has entered children's programming. It is therefore not surprising that in many countries, particularly low income, there is very little home-grown children's programming, educational or otherwise, and instead a predominance of imported foreign-origin programmes, often cartoons.

A variety of strategies have been adopted to stimulate the development of children's programming. First, a small number of countries have developed and followed well-articulated national policies for the development of television for children backed by government support in the form of public-service broadcasting on government stations or quota demands on commercial broadcasters. A survey of nine Asian countries, for example, found that China, Viet Nam and Japan had developed policies of this kind. Second, where children's broadcasting depends on imported children's programmes, then international agencies have sometimes played a role in funding the making of good programmes or funding their distribution. An international consortium of 70 animation studios, for example, was funded by UNICEF to produce broadcasts spots for 2,200 broadcasters in 160 countries based on different articles in the Convention on the Rights of the Child. These are intended for both children and adults. A third strategy is to produce programmes that can be used in a range of ways. For example, popular health and children's programmes can be broadcast at prime family times but can re-broadcast as schools' broadcasting and exploited in more child-appropriate extension activities. A fourth strategy is the using of commercial children's and family radio and television programmes as educational resources in themselves and the basis for children's media education.

Role of Internet Technologies

Industrialized, middle-income and even some least-developed countries have begun to find ways of providing schools with Internet links. Some are a long way down the road. In Slovenia, for example, more than 80 per cent of primary schools and 93 per cent of secondary schools have access to the Internet. Examples in developing countries include SchoolNet South Africa programme, a Uganda SchoolNet Pilot and the Enlaces project in Chile. The Enlaces project plans to connect 8,250 primary schools (50 per cent of the total in Chile) and 100 per cent of the 1,700 secondary schools by 2000. All these initiatives have required the deployment of hardware and arrangements for it to be serviced, acquiring software and making the necessary arrangements to train the teachers.

Once connected, children are using the web in a variety of ways. Websites for primary school learners and teachers offer a range of Internet-based educational services, such as discussion groups, and curriculum resources to download and use in the classroom. Many are dedicated to particular subject areas such as The Globe Programme (environment), The Wild Ones (conservation), TERC (mathematics and science). There are also examples of website design projects in which children themselves create resources to use and show. (e.g. DRIK Picture Library, Bangladesh).

A variety of on-line resources and courses have been developed that target adolescents in school, at the top end of the primary cycle or in junior secondary school. Some are ready-made materials that are posted on websites for downloading. Others involve opportunities for dialogue and collaboration between geographically separated learners in different teacher-learner and learner-learner combinations. The latter are referred to in a variety of ways – global classrooms, learning networks, virtual communities and e-mail classrooms. There are also examples of dedicated websites for in-and out-of-school youth. UNICEF's Voices of Youth offers a global e-mail discussion and opportunities for collaborative projects. It is sometimes possible to provide access to the Internet indirectly.

The Kothmale Community Radio in Sir Lanka, for example, uses radio as a gateway to the Internet for its rural listeners. Listeners, including primary school children and teachers, send requests (by post or on foot) to the broadcasters for specific information, about particular subjects. The broadcasters search for this on the Internet, download it and make the information available to their audience in a range of ways: constructing a broadcast around the information, sending the information by post, or placing the information in the radio station or in an open-access resource centre. This mediated access has several advantages: it can make the Internet's information resources available to rural and under-served communities; community re-broadcasting can relay the information in local languages as opposed, for example, to the dominant English language of the Internet; and the information can be pre-sifted, culturally mediated and presented to the audience in ways that are appropriate to local social practices.•

A different example of this mediated access is the growth of adopt-a-school projects. Schools, companies and individuals with Internet connections adopt under-resourced and unconnected primary schools in poor countries and solicit resources and funds on their behalf by setting up a dedicated website, with photos and needs-lists. Examples include adopt-a-rural-library schemes and, where language permits, send-a-comic and send-a-book campaigns.

School linking: One burgeoning use of the Internet is school linking – sometimes known as twinning – which involves the establishment of long- or short-term Internet links between individual schools for the purpose of communication between pupils, teachers, head teachers, managers and carers. Linking is occurring at regional, national and international levels in north-north, south-south and north-south configurations. At the moment, most linking occurs at secondary and junior secondary level but as computer provision is increasingly taken up at a primary level, links are beginning to be established between primary schools. For pupils, school linking opens up innovative and enriching learning possibilities: new learning communities, classroom pen-pals, information-sharing skills, resource exchange and development, collaborative writing and web-page development projects, and global virtual classrooms.

The global context can act as a powerful site for the 'recognition of, and support for, cultural difference' and for the assertion or protection of differences on the part of both parties in the exchange. In this, school linking appears to hold particular significance amongst minority and isolated communities such as setting up links within the Jewish Diaspora, between Afro-Americans and Africans, or among isolated Inuit and Native American communities. There appears to be considerable potential for expanding school linking in its different forms and particularly in promoting south-south links. They seem to be a successful way of building on and consolidating established links. The National Schools Network in South Africa, for example, was an extension of successful regional schools networks, a school-driven, grassroots networking organization.

Sharing resources: The Internet provides schools with the opportunity to offer more open learning opportunities through virtual courses. Virtual school projects, for example, commonly offer a range of Internet-based courses at junior secondary level, although these differ in the scale, structure and purpose. In some cases the virtual technologies are making it possible for schools to teach both on and off the school premises, replicating the mode of teaching of dual-mode institutions at tertiary level. Some allow students to study some courses on a face-to-face basis and others on an open-learning basis.

Electronic materials can in some cases be slotted into a face-to-face course as an additional resource. In other cases a full school programme is provided on either a face-to-face basis or on a distance-education basis for out-of-school learners, but both under the supervision of the school. In a third model, some schools have begun to offer on-line private tuition for home-based education, outside regular school provision and with the aid of parents. In practice the distinctions can become blurred; for example, when schools attempt to capitalize on virtual courses used in school by also offering them on a commercial basis to other learners.

Participation in some virtual projects provides schools with the means of extending their range of available courses without the need to expand enrolment or recruit specialist teaching staff. They are particularly useful as a means for increasing the access to a broader range of specialist subject courses in small and remote communities and without the need for learners to leave their home community. In some cases, groups of schools have worked together in this way in order to share their resources.

The Virtual High School (VHS), for example, is a recent co-operative venture between thirty-five high schools from twelve states in the United States in which they pool on-line courses and teaching-time. During the 1998/99 academic year, the schools offered forty NetCourses to students in the schools.

Courses include computer programming, music appreciation and composition, microbiology, stellar astronomy and statistics. Virtual High School teachers complete a graduate-level NetCourse to learn how to develop and deliver courses over the Internet with a view to them offering and hosting new courses. In exchange for teaching a NetCourse, schools can enrol students in any NetCourse being offered by other participating schools. In terms of technology, VHS uses 'interactive databases that teachers use to design their NetCourses' with students accessing 'their VHS Net-Courses using graphical web browsers like Netscape navigator or Microsoft Explorer'.

Another approach is to enable a central agency to develop materials for a group of schools. During 1995/96, the New Direction in Distance learning (NDDL) project of the Open Learning Agency's School Programme in the Canadian province of British Columbia delivered interactive instructional courses in mathematics, science, languages, humanities and applied skills to thirty-five learning sites, mostly in small high schools. The project was used to increase access to educational programmes in small and remote communities as well as to provide access to distributed learning models for urban schools and their students. Others were located in community learning centres so that the programme could also have implications for out-of-school adolescents.

By using a variety of network-based and more traditional distance- education tools, each course involves learners in both independent and group learning activities. Electronic communication occurs between geographically separated learners in using a range of technologies including computer conferencing, audiographic conferencing and web-based delivery. The choice of technology was influenced by the subject matter of the lesson. For mathematics, NDDL uses application-sharing whiteboards to teach mathematics when it is important for students to be able to see the instructor manipulate equations in real-time using hand-written figures and mathematical symbols.

A whiteboard is an electronic screen that resembles the classroom whiteboard. Learners at any site can see on their screen what someone at another site writes, and they can also write on, change and augment what has been written by others, hence the shared application feature. NDDL learners use small scanner (Visioneer Paperport) to digitise their homework assignments, then they attach file to e-mail, which is send to the instructor. The instructor uses graphic software to annotate and correct the assignments, which are then returned via e-mail to the learners, eliminating the expense and bother of paper transportation.

A total of 450 students completed courses during 1995/96. The programme was jointly funded by British Columbia Ministry of Education and the participating schools. In 1996/97, the fees were Can$1,000 per school district and $500 per NDDL school or community site. In addition, participating schools, parents or communities were expected to pay a tuition fee of $375 per student per course. The schools must also provide all the communications tools for student use. These include a local area network (LAN) connected to the Internet, graphics tablets, audio-teleconferencing equipment and various network and stand-alone software. Schools must also assign a site-based facilitator (either a teacher or paraprofessional) for one eighth of a full-time position for each 25 students enrolled.

NDDL supports teachers with a 3-day in-service course before commencing teaching duties and is currently digitising this training programme using videos and CD-ROM technologies so that new instructors, facilitators and learners can take initial training at their convenience any time of the year. The programme also supports students in job-seeking by providing on-line career counselling, job and work experience databases in the environmental and entrepreneurial fields.

E-Mail

Electronic mail is a very common form of online interaction, and is present in virtually every distance education package. It is also used as an adjunct tool for communication between teachers and students in many "face-to-face" courses. E-mail is a delivery and receipt mechanism mostly for textual material, although other files, which could be textual or any other type, can be "attached" to the message. It allows educators and students to communicate with each other asynchronously, sending messages to individuals or groups easily and quickly. Messages can be written at any time, and can be read and responded to at any time. A file of e-mail messages sent and received is typically archived on the individual's computer.

Threaded Discussions

Threaded discussions are another form of asynchronous textual communications. An educator or student may post a message pertaining to a certain subject in a forum accessible to the whole class. Other participants can respond to that message or any of the responses, and so on. The evolution of the threaded discussion is displayed in hierarchical form to allow a participant to follow the discussion. A student or instructor can read the original message, the responses it generated, and the further comments generated by each of those responses. In this way, it seeks to recreate, in a time-independent environment, the flow of a classroom discussion while keeping a record of the discussion's progress.

Chat

The chat function provides a synchronous meeting place online. Students and instructors who are online and in this program can write messages back and forth in real time. As one student types a message, for instance, the text appears on the computer of all the other students present in the chat room. This technology allows for live discussion similar to classroom experiences. It is possible for the participants to keep copies of the chat session.

Whiteboard

A whiteboard program is one that provides a common space in which students and instructors can work synchronously. Similar in use to a blackboard in class, whiteboard technology can be used for display or collaboration. During a whiteboard session, each participant has a blank application on their screen, a "whiteboard." Any participant can then cut, paste, draw or write anything into this common space, and it will be immediately displayed on the boards of all the other participants. This technology is useful for group projects or planning sessions, which require students to collaborate on creating something. It can also be used in connection with a lecture delivered through streaming technologies, permitting the instructor to display images or text to the class as she lectures. Participants can save the contents of the board to their computer at any time.

Shared Applications

Like the whiteboard, a shared application can be used for display or collaboration. A shared application is a computer program like a word processor or drawing program that permits several people to use the program at the same time from different locations. The participant with the program to be shared (usually the teacher) opens it and specifies that he wants to share it. Demonstrations can be accomplished this way or, if the instructor specifies that the application can be used for collaboration, anyone in the class can also use the shared application.

For example, all participants in a class session might have access to the same word processing program or graphic design program, and would work with each other within the application to create a product. In some implementations, the work that is done in the application can be saved or printed only from the computer of the person who shared it. For someone else to obtain a copy of the final product after collaborating, the person who shared it must send the file to the other participants.

Streaming Video/Audio

Streaming video or audio is similar to broadcast technologies. except that the transmissions are sent over a computer network. Instead of the receiving computer's waiting to receive an entire file of audio or video information before playing it back, the receiving computer begins to play back the file while it is still arriving over the network. Playback is done "on the fly," in other words. With enough network capacity ("bandwidth") the result is comparable to radio or television. In practice, however, the limits of the Internet's capacity today result in video images appearing small, with jerky movements. Sound quality is often quite good, though here again, the speed of one's connection to the Internet, and the congestion on the Internet at the time, make substantial differences in the quality of playback. In common implementations today, streaming audio and video do not result in a complete copy of the entire transmission being placed on the user's computer, although a different implementation could be created that would do so. With appropriate equipment, such as cameras and microphones, the audio or video can also be two-way. This technology is used to deliver lectures to students, or hold class sessions with interaction.

Video/Audio Files

Video and audio files can be used to illustrate lessons or teach specific subjects. For example, a foreign language class might contain sound clips of different pronunciations of words, or a history class might integrate video clips of recorded interviews of war survivors with the lecture material. These files reside on the class network site for the duration of the class, and can be copied and downloaded by the students.

Course Management

Course management describes the infrastructure of the instructional content of the course. This could include the syllabus, written or recorded lectures, assigned reading, tests, and homework assignments. It generally involves posting material in common spaces on the network site, together with directions on how and when to access different portions of the material. For instance, an instructor might post a new lecture every week, with reading assignments, and a subsequent threaded discussion on the lecture. Or, she might choose to post all lectures and reading material at the beginning of the course, allowing students to read ahead, and organize chat sessions or threaded discussions every week on a different lecture. This information, once posted, generally remains on the course site for the duration of the class.

Links

Links provide a way for students to quickly access material not present on the course site itself. Links to other websites can be embedded in the text, or listed separately. For instance, a lecture on computer programming might include a link to an Internet website rating different types of software. Links may also transport the student to the university's library, where a student may access electronic reserves of material put aside by the instructor for that particular class.

Interactive CD-ROMs and DVD-ROMs

Some classes furnish students with a CD-ROM or DVD-ROM that interacts with the course website. These store large files, such as video, audio or animation, that would otherwise be posted on the websites. When the student clicks on the graphic or video clip in the course site, his computer obtains the file straight from the CD-ROM or DVD-ROM, instead of downloading it from the web page. This saves time, and also allows large files to be viewed with higher quality. The above tools are generally used in classes that involve some form of instructor-student interaction. There are also tools available for self-paced independent learning-the latter-day parallel to video and audio tape courses that can be taken home and used at the student's convenience, with no interaction with a teacher. In the digital environment, computer-based training is a common form of distance education.

Programs on a variety of subjects can be obtained by the student from commercial vendors or in the course of instruction at an educational institution. The student reviews the material at his own pace, and tests himself on computer-generated exams. The programs themselves may contain a mixture of media, including video, audio, graphics and text. They could be contained in a CD-ROM, for example, downloaded from a network site, or accessed online. The student has little or no interaction with a teacher, although the student may send the results of the computer testing to an educational organization for grading or credit.

Outcomes of Technology Use in Education

We can expect outcomes to be of three kinds. Using new technologies in education may widen access and therefore move towards increased equity, or raise quality, or change the curriculum. Assessment of outcomes is complicated because each kind of change is likely to be marked by a different indicator. Thus, while we are critical of the scarcity of studies that demonstrate improvements in quality following the introduction of new teaching technologies, we may be falling into a category error in seeking them. If computers in the classroom change the nature of what children do, shift the process of their learning and mean they learn more of one skill and less of another, then comparative studies of learning gain or examination passes are of limited value.

Increasing Equity

There is a wealth of experience of the use of varied technologies in order to extend education. In principle communication technologies make it possible to reach out to audiences who cannot be brought into a school or adult learning centre. The potential for using technologies to widen access to education remains important today as it did over the past century. But in practice this experience tends to be piecemeal, under-reported and difficult to evaluate, and often on a modest scale. Furthermore, the dramatic stories about widening access tend to be low technology: BRAC and Escuela Nueva, for example, are essentially adaptations of conventional education rather than major uses of new technology. Projects using print and broadcasting have some solid achievements in widening access, especially at the level of junior secondary education. The well-established Telesecundaria project in Mexico was reaching over 750,000 students in 1997/98 in 12,000 centres, over 15 per cent of the total junior-secondary population. It was, therefore, providing an alternative system of education to children in rural areas where there were too few conventional junior-secondary schools.

The evidence on using similar methods in Africa and Asia is more equivocal. Study centres in Africa, which have historically enrolled significant proportions of the junior-secondary age-group, seem to be in decline. Malawi, for example, has decided to transform its distance-education based study centres into community schools. The Asian open schools propose to reach extremely large rural audiences. One Indian forecast suggested the system might reach 40 million students in ten years while Indonesia hoped to enrol 2 million by 2008-09. Existing numbers, are more modest and it remains to be seen whether expansion at the level forecast is a realistic objective.

The use of technologies will not, of itself, increase equity. There is a danger that the use of computer-based technologies may widen the gap between countries, and between richer and poorer citizens or regions within the same country. Metropolitan schools with computers – and children whose families have computers at home – are likely to be at an advantage as contrasted with the rural and poor. There, may, too be a widening of gender differences if boys successfully elbow girls away from computers. Where, as in Mexico and in the newer Asian open schools, technology is being used to widen access, it does so at the risk of creating two classes of schools – conventional for the more fortunate and more urban, and non-conventional, principally for the rural poor.Then, there is some evidence of the success of using distance-education methods to widen access at junior secondary level.

Raising Quality

Technologies have been used in two main ways to raise the quality of basic education, through the use of broadcasts in classrooms and through teacher education. While conventional school broadcasting remain under-researched, the various Interactive Radio Instruction projects have been researched and solid evidence has confirmed their effectiveness. Projects have raised the quality of learning, as measured by tests of learning gain. There is some evidence to suggest that children's attendance at school is improved through their participation in interactive radio. There is solid evidence, too, of the effectiveness of distance-teaching approaches, using a variety of technologies, for teacher education. A decade ago there was already wide experience of the use of distance education. Although we have relatively few studies that investigate the effectiveness of technology-based training on subsequent classroom performance, the limited data available are positive.

By and large, distance-education programmes do succeed in getting trainee teachers to pass their examinations. Where we have evidence on teaching performance, teachers trained at a distance compare adequately with those trained conventionally. Most of the cost evidence is consistent that, above a threshold in terms of numbers, teacher training at a distance costs less than conventional training.

Advance Curricular Change

Various technologies have been used to advance curricular change. This was one of the aims of many broadcasting projects and has been the motive for some computer-based initiatives. The evidence appears to show that the introduction of computer-related education can bring benefits to learners and may increase learning. We have, however, little comparative data that would enable us to choose between, say, various types of computer use or an expanded programme of broadcasting in terms of their comparative effects on student learning. The crude and simple answer must be that increasing expenditure on education is likely to improve its quality but we are some way from having a metric that will provide a simple economic measure for choosing one technology rather than another.

There is anecdotal evidence of shifts in classroom practice following the use of computers, much of it from industrialized countries. An important comparative review of computers in schools in Chile and Costa Rica found evidence of educational gains following from the carefully planned use of LOGO in the classroom. This project was, however, exceptional in that the 'programme, which was launched in 1987, was designed as a total system underpinned by constructivist pedagogy and the Logo programming language. Its goal has been to contribute to the transformation of Costa Rican education through changes in learning and teaching that are brought about by the use of computers. the training if teachers, and the excitement generated by children's self-directed learning, knowledge creation and problem solving'

Effectiveness of Rechnology Use in Education

Experience from a range of programmes and projects makes it possible to identify some conditions that apply regardless of the technology chosen. some of them. indeed. characteristics of successful educational innovation generally. The first condition, however, bears directly on the choice of technology. From television to computers. a consistent lesson is that education needs to build on the general state of development of technology in the society or community rather than lead it. Educational projects which have been at the leading edge of technology run into difficulties and are rarely sustained in the long-term. It is cheaper. and easier. to introduce a form of technology into education. and keep it working, where education is riding on the back of large-scale developments by governments or the private sector. Television works for education when it follows rather then precedes television for entertainment; computers in schools can be maintained once commercial and private use has expanded to the point where there is an established service industry.Then, a whole set of conditions have to do not with the technologies but with the support structures that go with them, essentially to do with people rather than with technology.

The effective deployment of technology – from the simplest use of cassette tapes to computer-based learning – demands that there are arrangements on the ground that will ensure the effective use of the technologies and of teaching materials made available through them. Producing and delivering materials does not by itself ensure that they are used effectively. Success is likely to depend on training, on devoting adequate human resources to the development of materials, and on the process and location of innovation.Technological innovations make two kinds of demand for training. As they demand new skills from existing teachers, they make an immediate demand for training and updating of the large number of teachers who will be involved in their use, and the smaller number who will move into new jobs as media producers, managers or software designers.

Recent experience in the north suggests, that effective computer-education projects, for example, demand as great an expenditure on training and software as on hardware. The second demand is for changes to the curriculum of pre-service teacher training. If information and communication technology is coming rapidly into the classroom today, its use needs to form part of the curriculum of the education of the teachers of tomorrow. A recurring theme of project and innovation literature is the need to devote enough – which often means more than originally planned – resources to the development of teaching materials such as broadcast scripts. distance-education materials or computer software. From the Indian SITE project on, it has seemed easier to accept large budgets for capital expenditure on hardware than to devote the resources needed for the production of quality software. Success demands adequate investment in software.

Materials development is almost certain to raise questions of language. Language policy can foster national unity and identification or re-emphasize division. The pressure to maximize audiences and so reduce unit costs means that teaching materials are likely to be developed in an international language. Instructions on using technology, on-screen or off-screen, are even more likely to be in an international language. Most often it will be English and those with inadequate English may be doubly excluded if new-style, technology-based, education demands a higher level of capacity in English than they command, or than was necessary for more conventional education. Success may depend on the location of responsibility for an innovation. Technological innovators face a dilemma. On the one hand, if an innovation, whether in school or out of school, is to be sustainable it needs to be accepted by the educational establishment and gain a sense of ownership among teachers, administrators and budget holders. But, on the other hand, conventional decision-making systems and ways of allocating budgets may restrict innovation. Regular schemes of service and conventional approaches to time allocation in terms of student-contact hours, for example, do not fit easily with the processes of developing teaching materials whether for computers, broadcasts or distance education. Successful technological innovation needs both adequate integration with the rest of education and a greater degree of freedom than is necessary for the day-to-day running of the more established parts of the education service.

The freedom to innovate needs to be accompanied by a sensitivity to those who will be affected by the innovation. Again, projects that are imposed, without consultation with beneficiaries and users, have been among the first to fail.Finally, technologies are seldom neutral in their effect: a sensitive process of consultation needs to take account of the possible effects of a technological innovation on issues of gender and of language. There are many examples - from the need for measures to prevent boys, in some northern cultures, getting more than their fair share of limited time on the keyboard to the planning of radio programmes of rural adult education at a time convenient for men but when women are cooking. Decisions about the use of information and communication technologies in education need to start with the curriculum and with decisions about the curricular purpose of a proposed technological change. Quite different approaches to investment in hardware, software and training are needed, say, for increasing computer awareness among all children at school or for permitting access by health auxiliaries to information on the Internet.

The early experiments with computers in schools were led by enthusiasts, usually in a handful of schools, and using the computer in a restricted range of subjects, sometimes, indeed, limited to 'computer studies' or 'information technology'. But projects of this kind may be a poor foundation on which to build, limited as they tend to be to a handful of favoured schools and leaving large areas of the curriculum and the country untouched.

A condition for national programmes is therefore likely to be a phased plan for introducing information technology into education that takes account of the availability of technical support – even in remote places – and considers the most appropriate use of resources if, say, schools can afford only one or at most two computers. At this level, the highest priority may be to use the computers to help overcome teachers' isolation and to increase their familiarity with the technologies rather than directly in the classroom. The plan will need to take account of the significant recurrent costs of regular computer use: for technical maintenance, for updating software and for the replacement of computers as planned obsolescence makes them decreasingly useful. Where they are used for school linking, or for access to the Internet, then costs for line charges and for an Internet service provider need to be added on.

A national plan for computers will also demand decisions on the purchase or development of computer software. If use is to be limited to generic software – such as spreadsheet or wordprocessing programs or occasional educational programs like LOGO – then programs will be available for purchase on the open market. They will demand adequate facility in English and will assume that students will develop the globalized skills demanded by universal software. It may be unrealistic to worry about their cultural appropriateness.If it is intended to use teaching programs, for computer-aided learning or simulations, for example, the choice is more complex. Again, it may be possible to import software, at present mainly developed in the industrialized north. regardless of its cultural appropriateness. Or, if the market and language group is big enough. it may be possible to embark on the local or national development of software. We have not been able to identify cases in which this has proved economically viable.

Training has proved to be a major constraint on the effective classroom use of computers. With limited availability of hardware and software, it may be unreasonable to expect teachers across all disciplines to acquire computer skills and go on to the harder questions about how to integrate them into the curriculum. But there is a case for introducing topics of this kind into teacher education so that the next generation of teachers has that kind of capacity and flexibility.

If broadcasting is to be effective, it demands access to airtime on a frequency that is available to listeners and at a time that is convenient to them. Even though the costs of broadcasting may look modest when compared with those of computer-based education, they demand significant resources and there is therefore likely to be pressure to maximize the audience in order to reduce the unit cost. One way of doing this is to develop broadcasts that will meet the needs of more than one audience – formal education in school and informal outside. Another is to repeat broadcasts so that the initial production costs are spread over a longer period and a larger audience. The early studies of interactive radio suggested that programmes might be used for up to ten years. In practice, as teachers have become familiar, or over-familiar, with existing radio lessons they have pressed for change and become unwilling simply to repeat, with a new class, old materials.

The effectiveness of distance education seems to turn on four factors. The first is good management and administration. Projects that have been based in a small, non-specialist institution have tended to be vulnerable. The most promising way forward may be to work with an open university or dedicated distance-teaching institution whose responsibilities include education at lower levels.Second, effectiveness depends on the development of good materials and, above all, on student support. Success may therefore depend on judicious expenditure on that part of a distance-education system where economies of scale are not possible.Third, evidence shows that motivation is all important. Programmes of teacher education using distance teaching have achieved impressive results and high successful completion rates, even with not very well-educated students, materials of mediocre quality and imperfect student-support systems, when students can expect promotion and more pay on completing their course. In contrast, adults and adolescents in programmes that are something like an alternative school, and without that promised reward, have much poorer success records. Fourth, for teacher education, it is imperative to develop links between what is done through distance education and the practical work of the teacher in the classroom. Unless the logistics of this kind of link are effective, distance-education programmes are likely to have only modest effects at best.

If technologies are to help towards quality education for all, then we need to consider their relevance to the problems of quantity and access, and to issues of quality, and to relevance of the curriculum to society's present and future needs. Pedagogy precedes technology.One common strand running through any analysis of the new technologies is the gap between the information-rich and the information-poor. The gap exists within countries, especially between town and country, and between countries and regions.

A priority for development in the new century is therefore to find strategies to bridge this gap. It will be ironical, if not tragic, if the benefits of reducing the costs of communication flow only to the rich and not the poor. Already there is a danger that the rich can communicate by e-mail and seek information from the Internet at negligible cost while the poor, with poorer access, still have to meet the greater costs of conventional post, fax and book supply. Resolving the problem will not be easy but neglecting to address it may be catastrophic.

We can examine the role of technology in relation to the characteristics of learners – from children to adults and intermediaries – and to the wealth of their society. We move now from the youngest and poorest to the oldest and richest. While there has long been an expectation that it might be possible to offer a technology- based, non-formal, alternative to primary schooling, there is little record of success to guide us here. But there are two important exceptions to this hesitation about technology.

First, many of the poorest and most remote schools also have the least qualified and experienced teachers. Teacher-edu-cation programmes, using whatever combinations of technology are available, are an effective way of raising school quality. Expenditure on technology for teachers, with its multiplier effect, is likely to be easier to justify than expenditure on technology in schools.

Second, the power of radio to raise the quality of teaching has been amply demonstrated as have its relatively modest unit costs. The new century could raise educational quality by an imaginative rediscovery of radio. With the approach of universal primary education, many countries will continue to face problems of access and quality, and problems arising from the shortage of suitably trained teachers, at junior-secondary level. Broadcasting projects and the important work of open schools in reaching out-of-school audiences of primary-school leavers have demonstrated that technologies can assist in the expansion of junior-secondary schooling. There is scope for programmes that hold down costs by using the same materials, and in part the same organizational structure, for audiences outside as well as within school.

It is more difficult to forecast, or to suggest guidance for, the development of computer-related activities within school. Forecasting is made particularly difficult because of the pace of technological change: 'computer education' may today be about access to information on the Internet while a few years ago it was about writing programs in basic.

The introduction of computers into the classroom can offer new opportunities for communication and for access to information. At the same time it may make heavy curricular demands, asking that aspects of information technology should be included in the regular curriculum and should, in consequence, displace something else. These are accompanied by demands for relevant teacher education and for significant continuing investment in hardware and software.

In industrialized countries the policy issues that arise are likely then to be tactical rather than strategic, about the student: computer ratio, about the balance between using computers as a means of communication or as a way of developing skills needed by students as part of a general education and about control of access to any information on the Internet.

Within middle-income and developing countries there is a tier of strategic questions about the minimum level of investment that is necessary for defined curricular purposes and about the most effective way of deploying computers if, say, there are to be only one or two in any school. Among the approaches that have been suggested are the introduction of computers on a phased and regional basis and their restriction to the upper levels of the education system. If schools have only a single computer, with limited Internet access or dependence on CD-ROMs, it is probably most appropriate to put the computer into the library where there is one and perhaps to concentrate on its use to overcome teacher isolation and for teacher in-service education. A further possibility is to encourage the use of computers within teachers' colleges and to explore whether it is possible to get shared use of, say, computer facilities provided to a telecentre or teachers' college.

Technology provides two kinds of opportunity for the education of adults.

First, as we have seen, there is a strong educational and economic case for the development of technology-based programmes to raise the effectiveness of intermediaries, including teachers, extension agents and health workers. Wherever attention is moving from pre-service to in-service teacher education, we see a major role for the use of communication media. Examples to guide us include the use of the Internet within teacher-training colleges, the many programmes of distance education for teachers and the experiments, in India and elsewhere, in using teleconferencing for teacher education.

Second, there is scope for an expansion of non-formal education, despite all the setbacks. The careful and planned use of mass media for large-scale programmes of public education justifies investment both because of potential direct benefit to the learners and because of the negative impact on the formal education system of their absence.New technologies and new organizational structures may have a role to play here. Indeed, as information on the Internet becomes more universally available, technology- based non-formal education may become ever more important.

Developing countries have the opportunity to leapfrog the industrialized, using technologies so that they develop a stronger system of education with-out going through the same slow stages of development that have been followed in the industrialized world. It was suggested at the time that the large-scale instructional television projects of the 1970s would allow developing countries to leapfrog industrialized ones and so accelerate their educational development. Television did not bring this result: a generation later we cannot point to any education system that was transformed as a result of investment in television rather than in teachers and blackboards, and in the slow process of raising teacher and school quality.

More recently there have been some examples of leapfrogging in communications technology. India and Thailand, for example, have used satellite broadcasting where industrialized-country broadcasting has till recently been dominated by terrestrial systems. Cellular telephones have spread rapidly in Ghana so that a cellular network is in place while the terrestrial one is still limited in its coverage.

Can we expect educational leapfrogging, in which a technology- dominated system of education can be established more rapidly and more economically than conventional approaches to strengthen education? Four conditions seem to be necessary for this to happen.

The first is that telecommunications should be capable of delivering the greater part of the curriculum: if they are only used for, say, a tenth of the time or the content then they do not allow for the significant reductions in expenditure on conventional education that would be necessary to make savings in unit costs. This condition may be met in higher education, where technology-based teaching has in a limited number of cases proved to be a viable and effective alternative. It may be met in large-scale, broadcast-based projects at junior secondary level, like Telesecundaria in Mexico, but it seems unlikely that it can be met at primary level. For both social and educational reasons, parents, teachers and politicians all expect that young children need to study, in a class-room and with a teacher, and do not believe that the technologies can provide an adequate substitute for this.

The second condition is that an adequate communications infrastructure is in place. Effective radio, for example, demands that schools should be able to afford radios, have access to mains electricity or to batteries and funds to pay for them, and to a service industry that will repair and replace radios when they break. A web-based computer education service demands reliable electricity and telephone lines and, again, a support service to maintain equipment.

The third condition is that there is the capacity to train teachers, or mentors or classroom assistants if they are to substitute for teachers. Several different elements make up this capacity: a teaching force whose background education is adequate for them to learn and apply new teaching skills: enough time for them to study on top of their day job of teaching; and a national or local structure to provide in-service teaching even for the most remote teacher.

The fourth condition is economic. If technology-based teaching is to yield any economies, then the cost per learning hour achieved through the use of technology must fall below that of conventional education. Data from France and the United States suggest that computer-based teaching there has costs of between $1 and $2 per student hour, which would compare favourably with the cost per hour of conventional teaching which is in the range $4 to $12.

But a large proportion of the costs for computer-based teaching are a function of the costs of the technology. These costs are likely to be as high in developing as in industrialized countries, or even higher. In contrast conventional costs per student reflect local wage rates for teachers and may be as low as $0.10 per hour within LDCs, a fraction of the cost to be expected for technology- based teaching. Orivel has suggested that it is only when countries are achieving a GNP per capita of $7,300 that they may reach a breakeven point in which computer-based costs match those of conventional education. Even here, if technology is to produce savings, it must substitute for teachers. For most LDCs technology can only increase the cost of basic schooling, not reduce it. If we focus on the needs of primary education in most developing countries, it is clear that none of the conditions for educational leapfrogging are likely to be met. Crucially, there are strict economic constraints on the deployment of technologies unless these are to replace teachers, to minimize costly interaction with a tutor, and to reach such large audiences that they achieve economies of scale.

There are ways in which the application of technology to basic education can help widen access, raise quality and in some circumstances contain costs. But the picture of technological development over the past decade is of piecemeal and hap-hazard development, with some successes, some failures, and many initiatives undertaken without evaluation and within a policy vacuum.

We can therefore conclude that sound development needs to take place within a national communication policy, one aspect of which will be a policy for the educational use of communications. In arguing this, it is assumed that a national communication policy will consider political, economic, technical and legal or regulatory issues. It will need to define the roles of the private and public sector in relation to the whole range of information and communication technologies. One key issue here may be a strategy to allow educational institutions access to telecommunications on favourable terms, possibly through the use of governments' regulatory powers in the telecommunications sector.

A communications policy will need to consider the following among other areas:

— policy on tariffs and on any common carrier requirements; investment policy, in relation both to the public sector and to the encouragement of particular areas of private-sector investment;

— government purchasing policy, and policy for the use of communication technologies for government's internal communication;

— technical standards including frequency allocation; the national development of capacity and expertise: issues of equity and access;

— intellectual property, seeking an appropriate balance between 'the right of creators to benefit from the use of their work and the needs of users to access those works and use them freely' .

3

Essentials of Web-based Education

Web-based education (WBE) is currently a hot research and development area. Benefits of Web-based education are clear: classroom independence and platform independence. Web courseware installed and supported in one place can be used by thousands of learners all over the world that are equipped with any kind of Internet-connected computer.

Thousands of Web-based courses and other educational applications have been made available on the Web within the last five years. The problem is that most of them are nothing more than a network of static hypertext pages. A challenging research goal is the development of advanced Web-based educational applications that can offer some amount of adaptivity and intelligence. These features are important for WBE applications since distance students usually work on their own (often from home).

An intelligent and personalized assistance that a teacher or a peer student can provide in a normal classroom situation is not easy to get. In addition, being adaptive is important for Webbased courseware because it has to be used by a much wider variety of students than any "standalone" educational application. A Web courseware that is designed with a particular class of users in mind may not suit other users.

The world market of online education and training estimated to be worth $19 million in 1995, is projected to be about $54.1 billion by 2005. This reason motivates many educational institutions in academia and industry to expand their activities on Web-based education and design and development of Web-based courseware.

The vast majority of the educational institutions worldwide actively use various Web-based instructional tools (WBI tools) of the 1st and 2nd generations for a design and development of Web-based curricula and courseware. However, the leading U.S. institutions such as Stanford University, Carnegie Mellon University, University of Illinois 0 Urbana-Champagne, University of Michigan - Ann Arbor, recently designed, developed, and started to actively use the WBI tools of the third generation in order to support the Web-Based Education (WBE) in their institutions. The InterLabs state-of-the-art agent-based Web-lecturing tool of the third generation has been designed, developed, and tested at the Department of Computer Science and Information Systems, and NSF-Bradley Center on Web-Based Education at Bradley University, IL, U.S.A., and used in several U.S. educational institutions, including Bradley University and Midstate College. It meets the requirements of the "active learning" paradigm of education, "student-centered" model of education and pedagogy of Web-based education and virtual colleges/universities.

The vast majority of the educational institutions worldwide actively use various Web-based instructional tools (WBI tools) of the 1st and 2nd generations for a design and development of Web-based courses.

WWW educational tools of the 1st generation are stand-alone tools such as email lists archiving. newsgroups. and bulletin boards (Hypernews, Eudora, Pegasus. etc.). static WWW pages (browsers: Netscape. Microsoft Internet Explorer), editors (HotDogPro. Visual Page, etc.), text -based conferencing tools (iChat, HyperChat. etc.). online file (Fetch. WS-FTP. CuteFTP), audio-only and audio/video conferencing (CU-SeeMe, Big Picture, Videum ConfPro, etc.). whiteboards (Microsoft NetMeeting, Netscape Communicator). special application environments (various Java applets. Gamelan. etc.).

WBI tools of the 2nd generation are integrated tools such as ToolBook Assistant/Librarian, AuthorWare. WebCT. Convene, BlackBoard, Director, FrontPage. and multiple other tools. However, the leading U.S. universities including Stanford University, MIT. Carnegie-Mellon University. University of Michigan – Ann Arbor, started to use the Web-based educational tools of the 3rdgeneration – the so-called Web-lecturing tools. Those tools usually comprise a) a streaming or pre-recorded "live" video- and audio. b) rich PowerPoint presentations, c) VCR control buttons for both audio/video and slides, and d) multiple "student-to-student" and "student-to-teacher" communication tools. The appropriate examples may include but are not limited to JITL. Stanford Online, MANIC, CALAT. AOF. Sync-O-Matic 3000. WLS, MStar, Classroom 2000, KMi Stadium. and CA309 tools.

Adaptive Web-based Education System

While many research papers and media publications report substantial success with Web-based education, a careful analysis of the situation and informal discussions with "on-line teachers" show that Web-based education is quite far from achieving its main goal - reaching a wide distance audience in a cost effective And educationally sound manner, and in particular accommodating the requirements of students from underrepresented groups.

Most of the positive experiences show that Web-based education works well for well-prepared, well-motivated students in reasonably homogeneous virtual classrooms. An example of a successful area are the masters-level courses for distance graduate students, certificate programs for students with college degrees, and various Web-based courses for sophomore/senior level students who take the course from the same or a remote campus.

Web-based teaching of freshman and junior level students who are less prepared and require a lot of attention from a teacher is more difficult. Currently the use of Computer Mediated Communication (CMC) tools to deliver instruction works well for in-campus students, who can visit teachers and assistants in office hours. The worst case is freshman and junior level distance students, who often are supposed to be the main audience for future Web-based education.

Current experience shows that distance education works here only when teachers and assistants can afford a lot of time for Web-based, e-mail, or telephone communication with their students (note that any Internet communication is still more time-consuming than real-time phone communication). This is not very encouraging.

Current "pioneer" distance students are still special - those who are already reasonably well prepared and motivated to register for a Web-based course, and for whom distance is the only problem (an example is high schools students earning their first credits). What needs to be changed in the current model of Web-based distance education to make it available for less prepared and less motivated students?

One of the difficulties with Web-based education is the course material which currently comes in various forms - lectures, tutorials, examples, quizzes, and assignments. In many current Web-based courses, the course material is still implicitly oriented for a traditional on-campus audience - reasonably homogeneous, reasonably well-prepared and well-motivated students who have access to teachers and assistants to fill possible gaps and resolve misunderstandings. However, Web-based courses are to be used by a much wider variety of users than any campus-based courses. These learners may have very different goals, backgrounds, knowledge levels, and learning capabilities.

A Web-based course which is designed with a particular class of users in mind (as it is usually done for on-campus courses) may not suit other users. The only way to enhance it is to make the course material richer and more flexible so that different students can get personalized content and a personalized order of presentation.

Current Web-based courses in this respect are not "flexible". In the best case, course material is a network of static hypertext pages with some media enhancement. Neither the teacher nor the delivery system can adapt the course presentation to different students. As a result, some students waste their time learning irrelevant or already known material, and some students fail to understand (or just misunderstand) the material and consequently overload a distance teacher with multiple questions and requests for additional information.

One suggestion is to develop Web-based courses which can adapt to users with very different backgrounds, prior knowledge of the subject and learning goals. For example, students with specific goals could get some parts of the course in more detail, students with some knowledge of the subject would not be taught the known material again, and less prepared students would get more examples and more problems, starting from the very simple.

We can distinguish three levels or steps of increasing complexity on the way to a flexible and adaptive courseware. The first level is to provide a well-designed hypermedia-based course containing all the required educational material: explanations, examples, tests, and problems for students with different learning abilities. The hypermedia interface makes it theoretically possible for each student to find his or her unique path through the hyperspace of learning material. This step could be made in many Web-based courses within the existing framework.

However, the first level is not enough for less-prepared students such as many college and university freshman and distance students. These users who have never worked with complex information systems simply cannot cope with advanced hyperspaces offered by modern Web-based applications. They will rarely be able to find a hyperspace path which is most relevant to their knowledge, background and goals.

The second step is to let teachers tune a generic course to the needs of particular students and classes by specifying a subset of topics to learn and the order of learning. The third step is to provide adaptive guidance mechanisms specially tailored to accommodate the current knowledge, learning goals, and information seeking tasks of that individual user.

Guidance in this context addresses the problem of a users' unproductive wandering, refocussing them on their learning objectives, suggesting logical next steps to inform them about the knowledge structure of the hyperspace, or re-sequencing materials according to their demonstrated knowledge of content. In these cases, the knowledge implicit in the hypermedia is well defined and carefully structured, similar to that found in a textbook. Adaptive guidance is especially important for Web-based courses because in many cases the user is "alone" working with it (probably from home). That is why "external" guidance, in which a colleague or a teacher typically provides adaptively in a normal classroom situation, is not available. We claim that all three steps up to the level of adaptive guidance must be made to turn Web-based education into a way to maximize educational opportunity for every type of learner.

A number of research groups worldwide are working now on adaptive Web-based applications driven by the importance of adaptivity in the context of Web-based education. Currently, two adaptive hypermedia technologies were used for providing adaptive Web-based course material: adaptive presentation, and adaptive navigation support.

Adaptive navigation support (ANS) is aimed to help students to find an "optimal path" through the hyperspace of learning material. The most popular forms of ANS on the Web are direct guidance, annotation, and disabling. Direct guidance was implemented in different forms in the following Web-based systems: ELM-ART-II, CALAT, InterBook, AST, Medtec, and DCG. Annotation was implemented in InterBook, WEST-KBNS, ELM-ART, and AST. Disabling was implemented in 2L670.

Adaptive presentation is aimed to adapt the page content to knowledge, goals, and other characteristics of an individual user. It is very important in WWW context where the same "page" has to suit to very different students. Only two systems implement full-fledged adaptive presentation: C-Book and 2L670.

One problem of all existing adaptive Web-based systems is that their development is quite time consuming. Until recently, any Web-based courseware development was time-consuming. Currently, a great variety of tools for developing Web-based courses is available. In addition to small specialized tools which are suitable for developing one of the course components mentioned above, there are many integrated tools which supports development of all course components. Here are just a few most well-known examples of university developed tools: WebCT, Virtual-U, CyberProf, Gentler, Albatros, FLAX and Mallard. A number of tools originally developed in universities are now commercially available. The most well-known commercial tools, TopClass and LearningSpace, are quite mature and used in many universities. The problem with all the above tools is that none of them supports development of truly adaptive courseware.

TopClass is capable of annotating, on an individual basis, folders as "unread" if they contain unvisited pages, or "new" if they contain new material. In this sense, and according to the definition of an adaptive hypermedia system, it is correct to describe TopClass as a weakly adaptive environment offering link annotation in a simple form. However, in this case there is no domain structure, that is, no indication of how information embedded in the pages is related.

Adaptive and Intelligent Technologies

Web-based Adaptive and Intelligent Educational Systems (AIES) are not an entirely new kind of systems. Historically, almost all Web-based AIES inherit from two earlier kinds of AIES: intelligent tutoring systems (ITS) and adaptive hypermedia systems. Most of adaptive and intelligent technologies applied in Web-based AIES systems were directly adopted from either the ITS area or the adaptive hypermedia area.

Table 1. Adaptive and intelligent technologies in Web-based educational systems that combine adaptive hypermedia and ITS functionality

System	Adaptive sequencing support	Adaptive navigation support	Problem solving	Intelligent solution analysis	Adaptive presentation
ELM-ART	Page	Annotation	Partial	Server	Some
ELM-ART-II	Course, tests	Annotation	Partial	Server	Some
PAT					
InterBook	Page, remedial	Annotation	Partial	Server	Some
VCProlog Tutor	Task, remedial	Server			

Table 2 Adaptive and intelligent technologies in Web-based adaptive hypermedia systems

System	Adaptive sequencing support	Adaptive navigation	Adaptive presentation
InterBook	Page	Annotation	Some
AST	Course	Annotation	Some
ADI	Course (knowledge+ interests)	Annotation	Some
ART-Web	Course,tests	Annotation	Some
ACE	Course (knowledge+ interests)	Annotation Hiding	Some
Remedial Multimedia System	Course, remedial	Hiding	
PT	Hiding		Yes
AHA		Annotation Hiding	Yes
WEST-KBNS		Annotation	
MetaLinks	Page		Some (intro)
KBS Hyperbook	Course	Annotation	

Table 3. Adaptive and intelligent technologies in Web-based ITS systems

System	Adaptive sequencing	Problem solving support	Intelligent solution analysis
CALAT	Course, remedial		
Medtec	Tasks		
Manic	Topic		
DCG	Course		
SIETTE	Question		
ILESA	Lesson, problems	Server. Java	
PAT-Online		Partial	Server
PAT-Java		Java	
WITS			Server
WITS-II			Server. Java
Belvedere		Server. Java	

ADIS (Yang-Akahori)	Server, Java	Server
D3-WWW-Trainer	Server, Java	
AlgeBrain	Server, Java	
ADELE	Server, Java	
TEMAI	Partial	Server, Java

As long as Web-based AIES research get more mature, it will produce original technologies inspired by the Web context. At least one of these Web-inspired technologies could already be identified (model matching). This section provides a review of existing technologies grouped by its origin. For each technology we list existing Webbased AIES and projects, which implements variations of this technology and discuss the ways to implement it on the Web.

ITS technologies

Intelligent tutoring systems is a traditional area of research that investigates problems of developing AIES. The goal of various ITS is the use the knowledge about the domain, the student, and about teaching strategies to support flexible individualized learning and tutoring. A review of existing intelligent tutoring systems performed by the author in 1990 helped to identify three core ITS technologies: curriculum sequencing, intelligent analysis of student's solutions, and interactive problem solving support.

All these technologies were implemented in numerous ITS. Since 1990, only one new technology (example-based problem solving support) was added to the set to classify a functionality that was not covered by the core three. While the proposed set of ITS technologies could be considered subjective and incomplete, it turned out to be very useful for classifying existing Web-based AIES. Web-based AIES that use traditional ITS technologies are usually called Web-based ITS. First Web-based ITS were reported in 1995-1996. These systems still constitute a rather small stream inside the ITS area.

Curriculum sequencing

The goal of the *curriculum sequencing* technology is to provide the student with the most suitable individually planned sequence of knowledge units to learn and sequence of learning tasks (examples, questions, problems, etc.) to work with. In other words, it helps the student to find an "optimal path" through the learning material. The classic example is the BIP system.

There are two essentially different kinds of sequencing: active and passive. Active sequencing implies a *learning goal* (a subset of domain concepts or topics to be mastered). Systems with active sequencing can build the best individual path to achieve the goal. Passive sequencing (which is also called *remediation*) is a reactive technology and does not require an active learning goal. It starts when the user is not able to solve a problem or answer a question (questions) correctly. Its goal is to offer the user a subset of available learning material, which can fill the gap in student's knowledge of resolve a misconception.

For active sequencing systems, it makes sense to distinguish systems with fixed and adjustable learning goal. Most of existing systems can guide their students to the fixed learning goal - the whole set of domain concepts. A few systems with adjustable learning goal let a teacher or a student to select a subset of the whole set of concepts as the current learning goal.

In most of ITS systems with sequencing it is possible to distinguish two levels of sequencing: high and low. High-level sequencing or *knowledge sequencing* determines next learning subgoal: next concept, set of concepts, topic, or lesson to be taught. Low-level sequencing or *task sequencing* determines next learning task (problem, example, test) within current subgoal. High and low level sequencing are often performed by different mechanisms.

In many ITS systems only one of these two mechanisms are intelligent, for example, a lesson is selected by a student, while learning tasks within this lesson are adaptively selected by the system. Some systems can only manipulate the order of task of one particular kind: usually problems or questions. In this case it could be also called problem or question sequencing.

Sequencing is currently the most popular technology in Web-based AIES. Almost all kinds of sequencing mentioned above were already implemented on the Web. Active sequencing is a dominated type of sequencing. Only a few systems (InterBook, PAT-InterBook, CALAT, VC Prolog Tutor, and Remedial Multimedia System) can perform passive remedial sequencing.Among active sequencing systems, only a handful of systems such as ELM-ART-II, AST, ADI, ART-Web, ACE, KBS-Hyperbook, and ILESA are able to perform intelligently both high and low level sequencing. Others, like Manic, leave a choice of activity within a topic to the user. Vice versa, some systems, like Medtec, leave a choice of a topic to the user but can generate an adaptive sequence of problems within the topic.

Most of the systems supports sequencing with fixed learning goal (equals to the whole course). Only a few systems support adjustable learning goals enabling a teacher (as in DCG) or a student (as in InterBook and KBS Hyperbook) to select an individual goal. The student can choose a goal as a subset of domain concepts (InterBook) or a project (KBS Hyperbook).

Active sequencing in most of the systems is driven by the students knowledge (more exactly, by the difference between student's knowledge and global goal). A few systems and projects, however, experiment with the use of students' preferences on the type and media of available learning material to drive sequencing of tasks within a topic. Two interesting cases of sequencing could be found in DCG and SIETTE systems.

DCG can perform advanced sequencing of educational material adapted to a learning goal. However, the sequencing is performed before students start working with the system producing a static Web-based course. SIETTE is an example of a Web-based adaptive testing system. The only kind of learning material it possesses is questions. The only thing it can do is to generate an adaptive sequence of questions to assess student's knowledge. Systems like SIETTE are incomplete by their nature and have to be used as components in distributed Web-based AIES.

While curriculum sequencing could be considered as the oldest ITS technology (it was implemented in almost all first ITS), for about 20 years it was a Cinderella among other technologies. Very little attention was devoted to it. Mainstream ITS research were centered around problem solving support technologies (which will be analyzed below). Problem solving support was considered as a main duty of an ITS, while delivery and sequencing of education material was though to be performed outside the system (usually. by a human teacher).

Naturally, almost no ITS includes educational material itself (other than a set of problems). The situation with Web-based AIES is very different. In the context of Web-based education a solid amount of educational material (usually structured as a hyperspace) is one of the main attractions of an educational system.

In this context (with its "lost in hyperspace" problem). curriculum sequencing technology becomes very important to guide the student through the hyperspace of available information. This technology is also natural and easy to implement on the Web: all knowledge could be located on the server and all sequencing could be done by a CGI-script. It's not surprising that, it is not only the oldest. but also the most popular technology of Web-based AIES.

Problem solving support technologies

For many years, problem solving support was considered as a main duty of an ITS system and a main value of an ITS technology. We have identified three problem solving support technologies:

— intelligent analysis of student solutions.

— interactive problem solving support. and

— example-based problem solving support.

All these technologies can help a student in a process of solving an educational problem. but they do it by different ways.

Intelligent analysis of student solutions deals with students' final answers to educational problems no matter how these answers were obtained. To be considered as intelligent, a solution analyzer has to decide whether the solution is correct or not, find out what exactly is wrong or incomplete, and possibly identify which missing or incorrect knowledge may be responsible for the error (the last functionality is referred as knowledge diagnosis).

Intelligent analyzers can provide the student with extensive error feedback and update the student model. The classic example is PROUST. As it could be seen from the Tables 1 and 3, a number of Web-based AIES implement intelligent analysis of student solutions.

Interactive problem solving support is a more recent and a move powerful technology. Instead of waiting for the final solution, this technology can provide a student with intelligent help on each step of problem solving. The level of help can vary: from signaling about a wrong step, to giving a hint, to executing the next step for the student. The systems which implement this technology (often referred to as *interactive tutors*) can watch the actions of the student, understand them, and use this understanding to provide help and to update the student model. The classic example is the LISP-TUTOR]. This technology is also represented by a number of Web-based AIES.

The example-based problem solving technology is the newest one. This technology is helping students to solve new problems not by articulating their errors, but by suggesting them relevant successful problem solving cases from their earlier experience (it could be examples explained to them or problems solved by them earlier). An example is ELM-

PE. In the Web context, this technology is implemented in ELM-ART and ELM-ART-II.

In the area of traditional ITS. the interactive problem solving support technology absolutely dominates. Interactive problem solving support is an ultimate goal of almost any ITS, while intelligent analysis of student solutions is often considered imperfect (and example based problem solving support is too rare to consider as a competitor). Again. the Web context changes the situation.

Both intelligent analysis of student solutions and example based problem solving support appears to be very natural and useful in Web context. Both technologies are passive (works by student request) and can be relatively easy implemented on the Web using a CGI interface. Moreover. an old standalone AIES, which uses these technologies, could be relatively easy ported to the Web by implementing a CGI gateway to the old standalone program. It is not surprising that these technologies were among the first implemented on the Web.

An important benefit of these two technologies in the Web context is their low interactivity: both usually require only one interaction between browser and server for a problem solving cycle. This is very important for the case of slow Internet connection. These technologies can provide intelligent support when a more interactive technology will be hardly useful. Currently, these technology dominates in Web context over more powerful and interaction hungry interactive problem solving support.

Interactive problem solving support technology is the last ITS technology migrated to the Web. The problem here is that the "fast-track" approach of implementing Web-based

ITS (developing a CGI interface to an older standalone ITS) used in pioneer systems does not work properly for this technology. It could be well illustrated by the PAT-Online system, which was probably the first trial to implement interactive problem solving support on the Web. This system uses a form-based CGI-AppleScript interface to a standalone Practical Algebra Tutor (PAT) system.

Since CGI interface is passive, the Web version of the system had to provide a "submit" button for the student to get the feedback from the system. Naturally, it also added another feature, which was essential for students with a slow Internet connection: a possibility to request a feedback once after performing several problem solving steps. As a result, PAT-Online moved to the category of an intelligent problem analyzers, more exactly, to a subcategory of analyzers that are capable to analyze incomplete solutions (ELM-ART also belongs to this subcategory). The intelligent analyzers of this subcategory can be placed between traditional analyzers and interactive tutors.

A real interactive tutor is expected to be not only interactive, but also active. It should not sleep from one help request to another, but instead should be able to monitor what the student is doing and instantly react to errors. It simply can't be implemented with the traditional server-side CGI interactivity and requires client-side interactivity based on Java. Java technology has matured very recently. Two years ago the review named it as a prospective platform for Webbased AIES and mentioned only three Java-based systems. Now Java provides a reliable solution for Web-based interactive tutors. To be more exact, Java offers two different solutions. One solution is a tutor implemented completely in

Java. It could be a Java applet working in a browser, or a Java application. Another solution is a distributed client-server tutor where a part of functionality is implemented in Java and works on the client side, and another part works on the server side. The parts communicate over the Internet. While the pure Java solution looks simpler (just a new language to build an AIES), the client-server architecture offers a more attractive choice for developing Web-based tutors. It is a definite choice for porting a standalone interactive tutor on the Web.

D3-WWW-Trainer and AlgeBrain demonstrate how to reuse the intelligent functionality of an earlier standalone tutor by changing it to a server-side application and developing a relatively thin "brainless" Java client that implements interface functions and communicates with an intelligent server. Event relatively small newly implemented interactive tutors such as ADIS and ILESA, which could be easily implemented in pure Java, can benefit from client-server architecture for such reasons as central student modeling. Finally, an overhead of the client-server approach (the need to have a distributed system) is not very big since Java naturally supports several ways of client-server communications - HTTP/CGI, sockets, or RMI/CORBA.

We think, that the client-server architecture will become very popular in the coming years as a standard way of implementing Web-based interactive tutors and a way to implement all kinds of highly interactive Web-based AIES. We already see examples of using it for implementing pen-based interface in WITS-II and an animated pedagogic agent Vincent in TEMAI.

Adaptive Hypermedia Technologies

Adaptive hypermedia is a relatively new research area. Adaptive hypermedia systems apply different forms of user models to adapt the content and the links of hypermedia pages to the user. We distinguish two major technologies in adaptive hypermedia: adaptive presentation and adaptive navigation support. Education always was one of the main application areas for adaptive hypermedia.

A number of standalone (i.e., non-Web-based) adaptive educational hypermedia systems was built between 1990 and 1996. First Web-based AIES that use adaptive hypermedia technologies were reported in 1996. Since that the Web has become the primary platform for developing educational adaptive hypermedia systems.

The goal of the *adaptive navigation support technology* is to support the student in hyperspace orientation and navigation by changing the appearance of visible links. Adaptive navigation support (ANS) can be considered as a generalization of curriculum sequencing technology in a hypermedia context. It shares the same goal - to help students to find an "optimal path" through the learning material. At the same time, adaptive navigation support has more options than traditional sequencing: it can guide the students both directly and indirectly.

In a WWW context where hypermedia is a basic organizational paradigm, adaptive navigation support can be used very naturally and efficiently. There are several known ways to adapt the links. Two examples of ANS-based standalone systems are ISIS-Tutor with adaptive hiding and adaptive annotation and Hypadapter with adaptive hiding and adaptive sorting. The three ways that are most popular in Web-based AIES are direct guidance, adaptive link annotation, and adaptive link hiding.

Direct guidance implies that the system informs the student which of the links on the current page will drive him or her to the "best" page in the hyperspace (which page is "best" is decided on the basis of student's current knowledge and learning goal). Often, if a link to the next best page is not presented on the current page, the system can generate a dynamic "next" link.

Adaptive navigation support with direct guidance is almost equivalent to curriculum sequencing technology. There are some differences though (in addition to the different origin). A page suggested by a direct guidance technology is always a page of the existing hyperspace. The student usually could reach this page in one or several steps without the system guidance. The guidance just helps the student to realize that this page is "best" and to get there fast.

In an ITS with adaptive sequencing a "page" with next best task or presentation could be completely generated from system's knowledge, thus the student has no ways to get to this material others than using sequencing. Also, direct guidance usually applies a one level sequencing mechanism (in comparison with two-level sequencing in most ITS): the best page is simply selected from theset of acceptable pages using some heuristics.

We refer to this way of sequencing as page sequencing. InterBook and ELM-ART provide good examples of this technology. However, the difference between these two technologies starts to disappear in the Web context. Web-based ITS systems are naturally moving to hypermedia platform representing at least some part of the learning material as a hyperspace.

As long as some type of educational material (presentations, problems, and questions) is represented as a set of nodes in hyperspace, sequencing of it becomes indistinguishable from direct guidance. To stress this similarity we have represented adaptive sequencing and adaptive navigation support with direct guidance in the same column of the tables.

The most popular form of ANS on the Web is annotation. It was used first in ELM-ART and since that applied in all descendants of ELM-ART such as InterBook, AST, ADI, ACE, and ART-Web as well as in some other systems such as WEST-KBNS and KBS HyperBook. ELM-ART and InterBook also use adaptive navigation support by sorting. Another popular technology is hiding and disabling (a variant of hiding that keeps link visible but does not let the user to proceed to the page behind the link if this page is not ready to be learned).

The options are either to make the link completely non-functional (nothing happens when the user clicks on it) as implemented, for example, the Remedial Multimedia System or to show the user a list of pages to be read before the goal page as done in Albatros.

Tables 1 and 2 list all major systems that use adaptive navigation support and indicates the type of adaptation. The goal of *the adaptive presentation technology* is to adapt the content of a hypermedia page to the user's goals, knowledge and other information stored in the user model. In a system with adaptive presentation, the pages are not static, but adaptively generated or assembled from pieces for each user. For example, with several adaptive presentation techniques, expert users receive more detailed and deep information, while novices receive more additional explanation. Adaptive presentation is very important in WWW context where the same "page" has to suit to very different students.

Only two Web-based AES implement full-fledged adaptive presentation: PT and AHA. Both these systems apply a flexible but low-level conditional text technique. Some other systems use adaptive presentation is special contexts. Medtec is able to generate adaptive summary of book chapters. MetaLinks can generate a special preface to a content page depending on where the student came from to this page. ELM-ART, AST, InterBook and other descendants of ELM-ART use adaptive presentation to provide adaptive insertable warnings about the educational status of a page. For example, if a page is not ready to be learned, ELM-ART and AST insert a textual warning at the end of it and InterBook inserts a warning image in a form of a red bar. A very interesting example of adaptive presentation is suggested in WebPersona project where an individualized presentation of information in an educational hypertext is performed by a life-like agent.

Web-inspired technologies

The last group of technologies is probably the most exciting one since these technologies has almost no roots in pre-internet educational systems. Currently this group include only one technology. We call this technology *student model matching* (or simply model matching) because the essence of this technology is the ability to analyze and match student models of many students at the same time.

Traditional adaptive and intelligent educational systems has no opportunity to explore this technology since they usually work with one student (and one student model) at a time. On the contrary, in the WBE context this opportunity happens naturally because student records are usually stored centrally on a server (at least for administrative reasons).

It provides an excellent framework for developing various adaptive and intelligent technologies that can make some use of matching student models of different students. So far, we have identified two examples of student model matching, which we call *adaptive* collaboration support and intelligent class monitoring. These examples quite differ from each other and probably could be considered as different technologies within the student model matching group.

Adaptive collaboration support is a very new adaptive technology which was developed within last 5 years along with development of networked educational systems. The goal of adaptive collaboration support is to use system's knowledge about different students to form a matching group for different kinds of collaboration.

The pioneering non-WBE (i.e., non-Web, or non-educational) examples of adaptive collaboration support are known for already a few years. These examples include forming a group for collaborative problem solving at a proper moment of time or finding the most competent peer to answer a question about a topic (i.e. finding a person with a model showing good knowledge of this topic).

Less than two years ago Brusilovsky predicted that adaptive collaboration support will become a popular technology. This prediction came true almost immediately. Now we can list already several real examples of adaptive collaboration support in WBE context. The group from University of Saskatchevan has extended their original workplace-oriented peer-help technology developed for PHelpS system to the WBE context in their Intelligent Helpdesk system.

Another similar system was developed and evaluated in the University of Central Florida. In addition to that, the group in the University of Duisburg known for their pioneering work on adaptive collaboration support have recently suggested a complete framework for implementation of intelligent support techniques for distributed internet-based education. This framework can naturally support their original adaptive collaboration support techniques and provides a framework for exploring other model matching techniques.

Intelligent class monitoring is also based on the ability to compare records of different students. However, instead of searching for a match, it search for a mismatch. The goal is to identify the students who have learning records essentially different from those of their peers. These students may be different from others in many ways. They cold be progressing too fast, or too slow, or simply have accessed much less material than others. In any case, these students need teacher's attention more than others - to challenge those who can, to provide more explanations for those who can't, and to push those who procrastinate. In a regular classroom the teacher can simply track students attendance and activity to find students who need special attention.

In a Web-based classroom, the teacher in the best case has only logging data - tables with numbers which are very hard to grasp. At the same time, the need to identify a small subset of students who need help more than others is more important. In WBE context, communication between teacher and students is usually more time consuming and a distance teacher simply can't individually address more than a small subset of the class. The system HyperClassroom provides an interesting example of using fuzzy mechanisms to identify deadlocked students in a WBE classroom.

Adaptive and intelligent technologies

It should be clear to anyone who is familiar with the needs of Web-based education, that adaptive and intelligent technologies can enhance different sides of Web-based educational systems. Adaptive presentation can improve the usability of course material presentation.

Adaptive navigation support and adaptive sequencing can be used for overall course control and for helping the student in selecting most relevant tests and assignments. Problem solving support and intelligent solution analysis can significantly improve the work with assignments providing both interactivity and intelligent feedback while taking a serious grading load from the teachers' shoulders. Model matching technologies can enforce both administration of distance courses and communication / collaboration between students and teachers.From another side, adaptive and intelligent technologies have not found yet their place in "real" virtual classroom, i.e., as a part of real courseware used by hundreds of distance students.

Most of the systems discussed above are typical "lab" systems, which have never been used for teaching real distance classes. The rest of them, a handful of systems mainly from ELM-ART and AHA families, were used in a few relatively small classes. At the same time, none of the dozens of commercial and "university-grown" Web courseware systems that are used in hundreds of real distance courses applies adaptive and intelligent technologies.

Web-based education itself is relatively young. Until now different companies producing Web-based education systems were able to compete on the market with their simple non-adaptive systems. However, a number of research level systems have already clearly demonstrated the benefits of adaptive and intelligent technologies. As long as the competition on the market of Web-based educational system will increase, "being adaptive" or "being intelligent" will become an important factor for winning the customers. Traditional Web-based education companies will start to include adaptive and intelligent functionality. Research teams with solid experience in using adaptive and intelligent technologies will found startup companies to bring their technology to the market.

The first technologies to be used in commercial systems will probably be sequencing technologies since they match very well to the current structure of Web-based education systems. Next will come the turn of adaptive navigation support and model matching. Problemsolving support technologies will stay on research level for longer, though we could expect the market debut of small Web-based tutors that are aimed to support teaching a fragment of some subject.

InterBook: A Tool for Developing Adaptive Web-based Courseware

InterBook is based on a specific concept-based approach suggested originally in and further elaborated by the ELM research group in the process of development an adaptive Web-based LISP textbook ELM-ART . ELMART happens to be one of the first and most influential adaptive educational system on the Web. A number of existing Web-based adaptive systems are based on the ELM-ART architecture. InterBook is an authoring system which implements this approach.

The current metaphor behind the InterBook approach is an electronic textbook (ET) which can be any hierarchically structured hypermedia material. An electronic textbook is also one of the most popular metaphors for representing online course material. Virtually any kind of course material can be represented as an electronic textbook.

Content representation

The InterBook approach uses two kinds of knowledge: knowledge about the domain being taught (represented in the form of a *domain model*) and knowledge about the students (represented in the form of individual *student models*). The domain model serves as a basis for structuring the content of an adaptive ET. We distinguish two content parts in an adaptive ET: a *glossary* and a *textbook* (or a shelf of textbooks).

The domain model and the student model. According to the InterBook approach, the keys to adaptivity in an adaptive ET are the domain model and the student model. The simplest form of domain model is just a set of domain concepts. What we call concepts are named differently in different research papers - topics, knowledge elements, objects, learning outcomes, but in all cases they are just elementary pieces of knowledge for the given domain. Depending on the domain and the application area, concepts can represent bigger or smaller pieces of domain knowledge.

A more advanced form of the domain model is a network, with nodes corresponding to domain concepts and links reflecting several kinds of relationships between concepts. This network represents the structure of the domain covered by a hypermedia system. The domain model provides a structure for representation of the student's knowledge of the subject.

For each domain model concept, an individual student's knowledge model stores some value which is an estimation of the student knowledge level of this concept. This type of model (called an overlay model) is powerful and flexible: it can independently measure the student's knowledge of different topics. The overlay student model can be kept up-to-date relatively easy.

All student actions (page visits, problem-solving, quizzes answering) are tracked and used to increase or decrease knowledge levels for involved concepts. Another component of the student model is the model of student's *learning goals*. Each student may have an individually assigned learning goal. A learning goal is just a set of concepts to be learned. A sequence of assigned learned goals forms an individual order of learning. Adaptive guidance mechanisms will ensure that the student achieves the first learning goal in a sequence, then the second one, and so forth. An individual order of learning is a convenient interface for the teacher to specify an individual syllabus for a student or a class. It may be done to adapt to special goals or backgrounds of the students, or to a particular textbook. An individual order of learning plus adaptive guidance are the mechanisms which are able to build an unlimited number of personalized adaptive courses from the same course material.

The glossary. The glossary is the central part of the ET. According to our approach, the glossary is considered as a visualized (and externalized) domain network. Each node of the domain network is represented by a node of the hyperspace, while the links between domain network nodes constitute main paths between hyperspace nodes. The structure of the glossary resembles the pedagogical structure of the domain knowledge and, vise versa, each glossary entry corresponds to one of the domain concepts.

The links between domain model concepts constitute navigation paths between glossary entries. Thus, the structure of the glossary resembles the pedagogic structure of the domain knowledge. In addition to providing a description of a concept, each glossary entry provides links to all book sections which introduce or require the concept. This means that the glossary integrates traditional features of an index and a glossary.

The indexed textbooks. InterBook represents educational material as a set of Electronic Textbooks. A human-written ET represents human teaching expertise on how to introduce the domain concepts to the learners. It is usually a real textbook represented in hypermedia form. Each ET is hierarchically structured into units of different level: chapters, sections, and subsections. Each terminal level unit is an atomic presentation, example, problem, or test.

Several ET on the same subject form a *bookshelf*. To make an ET "more intelligent" and to connect it to the glossary, we have to let the system know what each unit of the textbook is about. This is done by indexing of textbook units with domain model concepts. All books from the same bookshelf are indexed with the same set of domain model concepts. InterBook uses role-based indexing. Each terminal unit has an attached list of related concepts (we call this list *spectrum* of the unit). For each involved concept, the spectrum represents the name and the role of the concept in the unit.

Currently we support two roles: each concept can be either a *outcome* concept or a *prerequisite* concept. A concept is included in the spectrum as a outcome concept if some part of this unit presents the piece of knowledge designated by the concept. A concept is included in the spectrum as a prerequisite concept if a student has to know this concept to understand the content of the unit. Part of the InterBook approach is visualization of unit indexes, i.e., showing the set of outcome and prerequisite concepts of a unit on a *concept bar* to the right of the content of the unit.

Functionality

Domain model-based indexing is a relatively simple but powerful mechanism, because it provides the system with knowledge about the content of its pages: the system knows which concepts are presented on each page and which concepts have to be learned before starting to learn each page. It opens the path for several adaptation techniques presented in this subsection.

Advanced navigation. The knowledge about the domain and about the textbook content is used to serve a well-structured hyperspace. The system provides all regular navigation tools: sequential (forward/backward) and hierarchical (up/down) links within unit hierarchy, provides the navigation center for one-click transfer to all sections on the same or upper levels, and generates a table of contents where all entries are clickable links. In addition, it generates links between the glossary and the textbook.

The concept bar provides links from each textbook unit to corresponding glossary pages for each involved concept. On the other hand, from each glossary page describing a concept the system provides links to all textbook units which can be used to learn this concept. These links are not stored in an external format but generated on-the-fly by a special module which takes into account the student's current state of knowledge represented by the student model. This approach not only reduces page design time, but also provides the opportunity for direct guidance, adaptive navigation support, and prerequisite-based help.

Direct guidance and adaptive navigation support. The InterBook approach provides many more opportunities for browsing the course materials than traditional on-line textbooks. The negative side of this is that there is a higher risk for the student to get lost in this complex hyperspace. To support the student navigating through the course, the system uses adaptive annotation and direct guidance technologies.

Adaptive annotation means that the system uses visual cues (icons, fonts, colors) to show the type and the educational state of each link. Direct guidance means that the system can suggest to the student the next part of the material to be learned. Using the student model, it is possible to distinguish several educational states for each unit of ET: the content of a unit can be known to the student, ready to be learned, or not ready to be learned (the latter example means that some prerequisite knowledge is not yet learned). The icon and the font of each link presented to the student are computed dynamically from the individual student model. They always inform the student about the type and the educational state of the unit behind the link. In InterBook, red means not ready to be learned, green means ready and recommended, and white means no new information.

The same mechanism can be used to distinguish and show several levels of students knowledge of the concepts shown on the concept bar. In InterBook, no annotation means "unknown", a small checkmark means "known" (learning started), a medium checkmark means "learned" and a big checkmark means "well-learned". For many students, adaptive guidance provides enough support to make a navigation decision. Those who hesitate to make a choice could push the button "Teach me" and the system will apply several heuristics to select the most suitable node among those ready to be learned.

Prerequisite-based help. Prerequisite-based help is yet another adaptive guidance technique which is problem-driven rather than goal-driven. The system's knowledge about the course material comprises knowledge about what the prerequisite concepts are for any unit of the textbook. Often, when students have problems with understanding some explanation or example or solving a problem, the reason is that some prerequisite material is not understood well. In that case they can request prerequisite-based help (using a special button), and the system generates a list of links to all sections which present some information about background concepts of the current section. This list is adaptively sorted according to the student's knowledge as represented in the student model: more "helpful" sections are listed first. Here "helpful" means how informative the section is to learn about the background concepts.

For example, the section which presents information about an unknown background concept is more informative than a section presenting information about a known concept. A section which presents information about two unknown background concepts is more informative than a section presenting information about one concept. Prerequisite-based help is a very suitable technique to support student-driven learning. Students may have different interests in the same course and often jump far ahead in the course to reach the goal part of the material as far as possible. For these students, prerequisite-based help will support *backward learning mode*, i.e., starting from the goal portion of the course, learn the minimum background knowledge required to understand the goal part.

InterBook Aspects

This sections presents several aspects of InterBook: interface, implementation, and authoring. These aspects are secondary to the adaptive approach implemented in the Interbook. We can envision different interface and different implementations. In particular, authoring in InterBook could be significantly improved. At the same time, the information provided below is essential to complete a description of InterBook.

Interface

InterBook uses advanced features of modern browsers such as multiple windows and frames to provide the student with useful and powerful interface. Main windows used by InterBook are the textbook window and the glossary window. The Glossary window is used to view the glossary. The upper part of the window is a list of glossary concepts. The lower part of this window is used to show the glossary entry for a concept. For each concept the system presents the concept description (if provided by the author), the list of section titles (selected from all available textbooks) which present the concept (i.e., which have it as an outcome concept) and the list of section titles which require this concept (i.e., which have it as a background concept). Section titles are clickable links which makes the corresponding section to be loaded to the Textbook window.

The Textbook window is the most important window in InterBook interface. This window is designed to view the main content of a textbook, section by section. It is divided into frames performing different functions. Main frame of the Textbook window is the Text window. This window shows a particular section of the textbook which is called current section. For a terminal section the Text window shows the title of the section and the section itself. For a high-level section the Text window shows the title, the section preface (if existing) and the full table of content for the section (i.e. list of hierarchically structured titles of its subsections down to terminal level). A vertical bar to the right of the Text window is the Concept bar. It is used to show the concepts related with the current section.

All names of concepts on the Concept bar are links to the Glossary. The upper part of the Textbook window hosts the navigation center and the toolbox. The navigation center shows the position of the current section in the textbook: it lists the titles of all direct predecessors ("father", "grandfather", etc.) and all "brothers" of the current section. All names of the sections are clickable links. The navigation center serves for both orientation and navigation. The toolbox provides a set of buttons which are used to call additional windows (such as content window, search window, and prerequisite-based help window) which provides additional functionality.

Implementation

The WWW implementation of InterBook is based on the Common Lisp Hypermedia Server CLHTTP. CL-HTTP is a fully featured HTTP server completely implemented in Common LISP. CL-HTTP appears to be an optimal platform for our purposes. CL-HTTP offers a Common Gateway Interface to handle incoming URLs. To enable the server to respond to a particular URL, this URL has to be associated to a response function implemented in LISP. Answering an incoming request, the server recognizes a URL, calls an associated function, and passes the received URL and enclosed form values as parameters. In response, the function generates an HTML page. To do that, it can use a comprehensive library of HTML-generating functions. With such an architecture, CL-HTTP is a very flexible and powerful tool for implementing intelligent applications on WWW. Since a LISP function is called to handle the request, any interactive or intelligent tool written in LISP can be connected to WWW with the help of CL-HTTP.

Authoring

An Electronic Textbook is prepared as a specially structured Word file and the task is to convert this file into InterBook format. The result of this process is a file with the Textbook in InterBook format which can be served on WWW by the InterBook system.

InterBook recognizes the structure of the document through the use of headers. It means that the titles of the highest level sections should have a pre-defined text style "Header 1", the titles of its subsections should have a pre-defined paragraph style "Header 2", and so forth. The title of the textbook should have paragraph style "Title". The result of this step will be a properly structured MS Word file.

The second step in the authoring process then involves concept-based annotation of the Electronic Textbook (ET) to let InterBook know which concepts stand behind each section. This knowledge allows InterBook to help the reader of the ET in several ways, and the result of this step is an annotated structured MS Word file.

An annotation is a piece of text of special style and format inserted at the beginning of each section (between the section header and the first paragraph). Annotations have special character style (hidden + shadowed) which are not visible in the text window to the reader of the ET. For each unit the author provides a set of outcome and background concepts. In this way, each section is annotated with a set of prerequisite concepts (or terms which exist in other sections which should be read before the current section), and a set of outcome concepts (terms which will be assumed known once the reader has visited the section). The format for the outcome annotation is: (out: concept-name1, concept-name2, etc.) and the format for the background annotation is: (pre: concept-name1, concept-name2, etc.).

Once the annotations are complete the file is saved in RTF format. The RTFtoHTML program with some special settings is used to convert the ET into HTML format. Then the ".html "extension on the file is manually altered to ".inter" so that it can be recognized by the Interbook system.

Lastly, when the InterBook server starts, it parses all interbook files in its "Texts" folder (i.e. all files with extension .inter) and translates it into the list of section frames. Each unit frame contains the name and type of the unit, its spectrum, and its position in the original HTML file. The obtained LISP structure is used by InterBook to serve all the available textbooks on WWW providing the advanced navigation and adaptation features. The content which is presented to the student is generated on-the-fly using the knowledge about the textbook, the student model, and HTML fragments extracted from the original HTML file. These features of InterBook are based on the functionality of the Common Lisp Hypermedia Server.

Benchmarks for Succes in Web-based Education

It has been only 10 years since the coding language for the World Wide Web (WWW) was developed by Tim Berners-Lee in Switzerland, and Wide Area Information Servers and Gopher protocols became the first tools for "surfing the net." Since that time, educational institutions, research centers, libraries, government agencies, commercial enterprises, advocacy groups, and a multitude of individuals have rushed to connect to the Internet.

Internet and WWW profoundly influence society in general and colleges and universities in particular. Not since the printing press was invented by Johann Gutenberg in the

15th century has an "invention" generated such potential to change dramatically how people communicate and interact with one another.One of the consequences of this tremendous surge in online communication has been the rapid growth of technology-mediated distance learning at the higher education level.

A recent survey by the U.S. Department of Education's National Center for Education Statistics (NCES) found that from 1994-95 to 1997-98 the number of distance education degree programs increased by 72 percent. Moreover, an additional 20 percent of the institutions surveyed plan to establish distance education programs within the next three years. The survey estimated that more than 1.6 million students were enrolled in distance education courses in 1997-98, a number that is surely even higher today.

This extraordinary growth of technology-mediated distance learning in higher education has prompted several different organizations to develop principles, guidelines, or benchmarks to ensure quality distance education. These organizations include the American Council on Education, the National Education Association, the Global Alliance for Transnational Education (GATE), the Southern Regional Electronic Campus, the Commission on Higher Education of the Middle States Association of Colleges and Schools, and the Western Cooperative for Educational Telecommunications, among others. The quality assurance benchmarks promoted by these organizations are designed to apply to a wide variety of institutional contexts and consist of fairly broad statements. Virtually all of the strategies include such topics as course development, faculty training, student services, learning resources, infrastructure, and outcomes assessment.

These benchmarks, which were developed initially for all types of distance learning, have been in existence in various forms for a number of years. The question that arises is whether they are applicable to *Internetbased* distance education. In short, are the current benchmarks appropriate and necessary to ensure quality Internet-based distance education? Two organizations—the National Education Association (NEA), the nation's largest professional association of higher education faculty, and Blackboard Inc., a widely used platform provider for online education—are interested in exploring these issues and their implications. As a result, the two organizations jointly commissioned The Institute for Higher Education Policy to examine the benchmarks by studying active distance learning programs at several institutions.

The Institute was approached by the two commissioning organizations in part because of its previous experience in analyzing issues related to quality in distance education. The Institute's widely cited 1999 report, What's the Difference? A Review of Contemporary Research on the Effectiveness of Distance Learning in Higher *Education*, has generated considerable dialogue throughout academia about what constitutes quality in distance learning settings.

Specifically, NEA and Blackboard Inc. asked The Institute to attempt to validate those benchmarks that have been published by various entities, with specific attention to Internet-based distance education. Given the rapid growth of Internet-based distance education, how realistic are the benchmarks? Do they make sense to practitioners of Internet-based distance education? Are they taken seriously by higher education institutions? To what extent are the benchmarks being incorporated into institutions' distance learning operations? Are there additional benchmarks that are not found in the literature but are being used by practitioners that can contribute to the quality of distance education?

The study was designed to answer these questions by ascertaining the degree to which the`benchmarks are actually being incorporated in the policies, procedures, and practices of colleges and universities that are distance education leaders. In addition, the case study seeks to determine *how important* the benchmarks are to the institutions' faculty, administrators, and students. The results of the may assist policymakers—such as college and university presidents and chief academic officers, state coordinating boards, accrediting bodies, state legislatures, and governors' offices—as well as faculty and students, in making reasonable and informed judgments with regard to the quality of Internet-based distance education.

A case study addressing quality benchmarks for Internetbased distance education inherently includes some of the very limitations noted in the *What's the Difference?* report. The major conclusion of the report was that the research to date addressing the quality of distance education was inconclusive and, thus, much is still unknown regarding how, and in what ways, technology can enhance the teaching/learning process.

Internet-based distance education was a specific focus of the case study for at least three reasons. First, Internetbased distance education is quickly becoming the predominant technology in distance education, which is not surprising given the accelerating power of personal computers, increasing telecommunications bandwidth capabilities, and state-of-the-art software development and delivery.

The recent NCES report shows that not only is Internet-based distance education the most prevalent technology, it is also the fastest growing. At least 58 percent of the reporting institutions who offered distance education used Internet-based courses, compared to 54 percent who used two-way interactive video and 47 percent who used one-way pre-recorded video. Even as the percentage of institutions offering Internet-based courses3 jumped from approximately 22 percent to 58 percent in three years, use of all of the other technologies actually had declined since 1994-95. The report notes that Internet-based distance education will be a growing avenue for technology-mediated learning in the coming years.

In addition to the Internet's profound influence on distance education, it is also important to point out that a growing number of faculty are using the Internet to complement traditional classroom-based courses. For instance, it is not uncommon for course syllabi to be placed on the Web. Faculty also are using cyberspace to provide access to threaded discussions, group activities, and quizzes for their on-campus students.

Second, Internet-based distance education allows the teaching/learning process to occur "at any time and any place." The ability to provide asynchronous interactive learning activities has become the signature characteristic of this technology, setting it apart from most of the other technologies. Not only does Internet-based instruction allow the teacher and learner to communicate over any distance to any place, it alters the concept of time. Generally, students can participate in a course at any time of day or night they choose. Indeed, because of this characteristic, the term "24-7" has become a part of the lexicon of distance education.

Third, because of these features, Internet-based distance education is, in many ways, fundamentally different than traditional classroom-based education. Among other things, it is this distinctly different concept of time that engenders concern and skepticism from many in the higher education community. For some, though, it offers exciting new opportunities to teach students, as evidenced by the following observation from the League for Innovation in the Community College:

> The beauty of the Web is that it provides an entirely new context for teaching and learning. It removes the physical and time constraints for *instructors* as well as learners. Moving a course to the Web presents the perfect opportunity to return to the core principles of teaching and learning to create a new pedagogical model for our practices.

How can a teaching/learning process that deviates so markedly from what has been practiced for hundreds of years embody quality education? This question has been addressed in many ways by the range of benchmarks developed by a variety of organizations concerned about quality distance education. These benchmarks are examined in more detail in the following pages.

A Case Study

The case study process consisted of three sequential phases. First, a comprehensive literature search was conducted to compile those benchmarks recommended by several organizations, as well as those suggested in various articles and publications. Second, institutions were identified that have substantial experience and are providing leadership in distance education. Third, these institutions were visited by Institute staff to assess the degree to which the campuses incorporated the benchmarks in their Internet-based distance learning courses and programs. A more detailed explanation of each phase of the case study follows.

Phase I: Review of the Literature

In addition to reviewing benchmarks that have been published by policy and educational organizations, several articles by prominent authors in distance education were examined. Considerable overlap existed among the benchmarks developed by the various sources and, consequently, 45 specific benchmarks were identified. These benchmarks were grouped into the following seven categories:

— *Institutional Support.* The benchmarks in this category include those activities by the institution that help to ensure an environment conducive to maintaining quality distance education, as well as policies that encourage the development of Internet-based teaching and learning. These benchmarks address technological infrastructure issues, a technology plan, and professional incentives for faculty.

— *Course Development.* This category includes benchmarks for the development of courseware, which is produced largely either by individual faculty (or groups of faculty members) on campus, subject experts in organizations, and/or commercial enterprises.

— *Teaching/Learning Process.* This category addresses the array of activities related to pedagogy, the art of teaching. Included in this category are process benchmarks involving interactivity, collaboration, and modular learning.

— *Course Structure*. The benchmarks in this category address those policies and procedures that support and relate to the teaching/learning process. They include course objectives, availability of library resources, types of materials provided to students, response time to students, and student expectations.

— *Student Support*. This category includes the array of student services normally found on a college campus including admissions, financial aid, etc.—as well as student training and assistance while using the Internet.

— *Faculty Support*. Since not every faculty member possesses the skills and temperament for Internetbased distance learning, these benchmarks address activities that assist faculty in teaching online, including policies for faculty transition help as well as continuing assistance throughout the teaching period.

— *Evaluation and Assessment*. The benchmarks in this category relate to policies and procedures that address how, or if, the institution evaluates Internet-based distance learning. They include outcomes assessment and data collection.

Phase II: Identification of Institutions

Six institutions were identified for site visits. To qualify for selection the institutions (1) must have substantial experience in distance education; (2) are recognized as among the leaders in distance education; (3) are regionally accredited; and (4) offer more than one degree program via online distance learning. To ensure that a broad spectrum of higher education institutions were represented, the case study included a community college, a comprehensive institution, a research institution, and a virtual institution. The following institutions participated in the case study:

— *Brevard Community College.* This Florida college began offering distance education courses in 1974 and is also a participant in the PBS Adult Learning Service "Going the Distance Program." Brevard received a grant from the U.S. Department of Education's Fund for the Improvement of Postsecondary Education for faculty training and development in order to positively impact student learning.

— *Regents College.* This unique institution began in 1971 as the External Degree Program of the University of the State of New York. Focusing on working adults, the college offers online graduate programs in Nursing and Liberal Studies. Over 83,000 people worldwide have earned a college degree through Regents' programs.

— *University of Illinois at Urbana-Champaign.* As one of three participants in the University of Illinois Online, the institution offers 20 degree- or certificate-programs over the Internet, with more in development. The university received a grant from the Pew Grant Program of Course Redesign in 1999 to redesign a two-course sequence in Economic Statistics.

— *University of Maryland University College.* This virtual institution was founded with the mission of providing continuing education to Maryland's professional workforce. With over 25 years experience in distance education, the college offers14 bachelor's and 10 master's degree programs online. The college has twice been awarded the University Continuing Education Association's Award for Innovative Distance Education.

— *Utah State University.* This institution has been involved in various forms of distance education since 1911. The university offers two types of online courses, semester-based and independent study, and has been selected as a participant in the federal Learning Anytime Anywhere Partnerships program created in the 1998 reauthorization of the Higher Education Act.

— *Weber State University (WSU).* This comprehensive institution launched WSU Online in 1997 and currently offers two-thirds of the online learning courses in Utah. WSU received an Innovation in Distance Education Award from the University Continuing Education Association in 1998.

Phase III: The Institutional Visit

Between September 1999 and January 2000, Institute staff visited each institution. In addition to conducting indepth interviews with faculty, administrators, and students, a survey using a Likert Scale6 was administered to each interviewee. The survey also was administered to distance education students who were not able to participate in the interview process primarily because they did not reside near the institution. In all, 27 faculty, 62 administrators, 16 individuals who were both a faculty member and an administrator, and 42 students were interviewed and/or completed a survey, for a total of 147 respondents.

The Likert Scale listed the 45 benchmarks and requested each person to rank each benchmark on two criteria. First, to what extent is the benchmark true for the distance learning program (ranked from 1=completely absent to 7=completely present)? Second, how important is each benchmark to ensure quality (ranked from 1=not important to 5=very important)? Those persons who did not have sufficient knowledge or experience relating to the benchmark could check a "Not Applicable" box. The mean score, mode, and standard deviation were computed for each benchmark.

At the extremes, this process could result in four hypothetical scenarios: a benchmark could be present completely and very important; a benchmark could be present completely and not important; a benchmark could be absent completely and very important; and a benchmark could be absent completely and not important.

Benchmarks Identified from the Literature Institutional Support

1. Faculty are provided professional incentives for innovative practices to encourage development of distance learning courses.
2. There are institutional rewards for the effective teaching of distance learning courses.
3. A documented technology plan is in place to ensure quality standards.
4. Electronic security measures are in place to ensure the integrity and validity of information.
5. Support for building and maintaining the distance education infrastructure is addressed by a centralized system.

Course Development

6. Distance learning course development must be approved through a broad peer review process.

7. Guidelines exist regarding minimum standards for course development, design, and delivery.

8. Course design is managed by teams comprised of faculty, content experts, instructional designers, technical experts, and evaluation personnel.

9. During course development, the various learning styles of students are considered.

10. Assessment instruments are used to ascertain the specific learning styles of students, which then determine the type of course delivery.

11. Courses are designed with a consistent structure, easily discernable to students of varying learning styles.

12. The technology being used to deliver course content is based on learning outcomes.

13. Instructional materials are reviewed periodically to ensure they meet program standards.

Teaching/Learning Process

14. Student interaction with faculty is facilitated through a variety of ways.

15. Student interaction with other students is facilitated through a variety of ways.

16. Feedback to student assignments and questions is provided in a timely manner.

17. Feedback to students is provided in a manner that is constructive and non-threatening.

18. Courses are separated into self-contained segments (modules) that can be used to assess student mastery before moving forward in the course or program.

19. The modules/segments are of varying lengths determined by the complexity of learning outcomes.

20. Each module/segment requires students to engage themselves in analysis, synthesis, and evaluation as part of their course assignments.

21. Class voice-mail and/or e-mail systems are provided to encourage students to work with each other and their instructor(s).

22. Courses are designed to require students to work in groups utilizing problem-solving activities in order to develop topic understanding.

23. Course materials promote collaboration among students.

Course Structure

24. Students are provided with supplemental course information that outlines course objectives, concepts, and ideas.

25. Specific expectations are set for students with respect to a minimum amount of time per week for study and homework assignments.

26. Faculty are required to grade and return all assignments within a certain time period.

27. Sufficient library resources are made available to the students.
28. Students are instructed in the proper methods of effective research, including assessment of resource validity.
29. Before starting the program, students are advised about the program to determine if they have the selfmotivation and commitment to learn at a distance.
30. Learning outcomes for each course are summarized in a clearly written, straightforward statement.

Student Support

31. Students can obtain assistance to help them use electronically accessed data successfully.
32. Students are provided with hands-on training and information to aid them in securing material through electronic databases, interlibrary loans, government archives, news services, etc.
33. Written information is supplied to the student about the program.
34. Easily accessible technical assistance is available to all students throughout the duration of the course/program.
35. A structured system is in place to address student complaints.

Faculty Support

36. Technical assistance in course development is available to faculty and they are encouraged to use it.

37. Faculty members are assisted in the transition from classroom teaching to distance instruction and are assessed in the process.
38. There are peer mentoring resources available to faculty members teaching distance courses.
39. Distance instructor training continues throughout the progression of the online class.
40. Faculty members are provided with written resources to deal with issues arising from student use of electronically-accessed data.

Evaluation and Assessment

41. The program's educational effectiveness is measured using several methods.
42. An evaluation process is used to improve the teaching/ learning process.
43. Specific standards are in place to compare and improve learning outcomes.
44. Data on enrollment, costs, and successful/ innovative uses of technology are used to evaluate program effectiveness.
45. Intended learning outcomes are regularly reviewed to ensure clarity, utility, and appropriateness.

Rating the Benchmarks

It was clear from the site visits that quality benchmarks were considered with great care and embraced by every institution that participated in the case study. At every campus, at least one faculty member, administrator, or often several students stated that the benchmarks were on target and need to be addressed to ensure quality in Internetbased distance education courses and programs. As one respondent said about the survey, "Good questions. While the 'best' possible program would have rated *all* of these items as very important and strongly agree, one must consider resources and growing pains so as to target the *most* important areas."

In addition, several respondents were somewhat chagrined that Internet-based distance education was under such intense scrutiny while the traditional classroom-based teaching was not under the same spotlight. One person showed her exasperation by writing, "The same standards and benchmarks we use in distance education should be applied to on-campus courses as well. It doesn't happen that way here or across the country."

Because the intention of the case study is to validate the benchmarks for the higher education community in general, it serves no purpose to separate the data for each institution. While there are exceptions to the conclusions and comments from the interviews, the following discussion represents a consensus of a majority of the institutions in the case study. It is, therefore, not appropriate to assume that the attributes outlined in the discussion always represent each and every institution.

The information for the case study is both quantitative (the survey using a Likert Scale) and qualitative (the indepth interviews). No effort was made to apply any statistical tests to ascertain the degree of importance of a benchmark and its presence at the institutions, and the difference between the two. Instead, the more than 100 interviews (all lasting at least an hour) guided the analysis. The respondents were interviewed after completing the survey and many of their comments were directed to specific items in the survey. The interviews informed the quantitative data and served to put a "human face" on the stark numbers.

There are seven categories of benchmarks: Institutional Support, Course Development, Teaching/Learning Process, Course Structure, Student Support, Faculty Support, and Evaluation and Assessment. Each category is accompanied by a chart showing the relationship between the degree of presence for the benchmark and its importance to the institution. The discussion of the category includes comments from the interviews.

Institutional Support

All of the benchmarks in this category were considered important to ensure quality Internet-based distance education. The benchmark addressing electronic security measures received exceptionally high ratings both with regard to importance and presence at the institution. There was a marked difference between the importance of the benchmark regarding a documented technology plan and the actual presence of a plan on campus.

Respondents at some institutions complained that because of the extraordinary growth of Internet-based Compelling student demand has other consequences with regard to planning. Because of increasing student interest in Internet-based distance education at some of the institutions in the case study, administrators revealed that policies are being developed to catch up with practice. One administrator said simply that the institution is moving ahead without all of the answers. While some institutions were farther ahead in their planning than others, some institutions that are struggling to keep up with the demand for Internetbased courses have made a conscious decision to serve students immediately and plan later.

There is a substantial difference between the importance of the benchmarks concerning professional incentives and institutional rewards and their presence on campus. While considered very important, rewarding and providing incentives to faculty for good online teaching did not receive high scores with regard to their presence at the institutions. This conclusion was reinforced in the interviews, as revealed by comments from one faculty member: "We operate on a 'shoestring,' and the tenure, promotion, and reward system does not take into account the extra time a faculty member needs to teach well in distance education courses." Another administrator noted that at his institution, distance education "has some of our better instructors even though the rewards have not been there for them."

The dedication and knowledge of the faculty who teach Internet-based distance education was apparent in the structured interviews. The faculty who were interviewed showed keen insights into the teaching/learning process, and many were considered by their peers as some of the best teachers at the institution.

The high number of excellent faculty teaching Internet-based distance education courses can be explained partially by the faculty selection practice of many of the institutions. With few exceptions, faculty volunteered to teach distance education courses. One institution used the phrase "work with the willing" to explain this faculty selection process. Faculty who came forward, irrespective of the course they wished to teach, were often allowed to develop a course. Frequently these faculty were veteran teachers who were eager to teach using the Internet. This selection process, of course, produces an array of courses that may not necessarily represent a strategic plan of course and programmatic offerings. This is not to suggest, however, that Internet courses are generated without planning or strategy. As one administrator put it, "...although this institution did not have a strategic plan, 'strategic thinking' was used in the development of Internet courses and programs." For instance, several institutions attempted to develop Internet offerings for courses that had high enrollments such as lowerdivision, general education courses.

Many respondents suggested that a new benchmark should be added to the list: "The reliability of the technology delivery system should be as failsafe as possible." They explained its importance this way: "If the lights go out in a traditional classroom, it may be an inconvenience. If the system crashes, it's a calamity!"

Course Development

The three benchmarks relating to learning styles received a mixed reaction from the respondents. Benchmarks 9 and 11 were not considered very important and did not have a high degree of presence at the institutions. Benchmark 10 received low scores with respect to both importance and presence. The interviews helped to explain these sentiments. Many faculty and administrators stated that while these learning style benchmarks sound good on paper, actually meeting the standard is very difficult. One faculty member suggested that the research on learning styles is very poor and simply may not be an appropriate criterion for benchmarks.

The benchmark addressing the management of course design, also received a mixed reaction. By and large, the development of a course was the responsibility of individual academic departments and the extent to which the procedure met the criteria in the benchmark was a departmental decision. One faculty member said, "Some of the items suggest that greater evaluation, oversight, and course development ought to take place in distance education than for traditionally delivered courses. I don't buy this assumption. Traditional courses rarely come under that kind of scrutiny on this campus or others."

The notion of broad peer review generated many comments. The benchmark on the approval of course development was not considered very important and did not show a high degree of presence. There was considerable concern regarding the meaning of "broad." Many respondents made it very clear that peer review is, and should be, similar to the traditional model primarily at the departmental level. As one respondent explained, "Quality control is a department responsibility; additional requirements may endanger academic freedom and shared governance."

It is important to note that a possible disparity exists between the technology that an institution might possess and the technology available to the typical student. Although institutions may have enhanced, or are enhancing, their capability with high speed networks with additional bandwidth, and improved video quality, course development must take into consideration the technology that the students possess.

Many students have older personal computers, equipped with slow modems, insufficient memory, and small hard drives. Put more bluntly by one administrator, "Bells and whistles have to be available and understood by both the teacher and the student." The disparity between the technological capabilities of the institution and its students was referred to as "cutting edge, not bleeding edge" by one interviewee, while another referred to the "trailing edge" of technology.

Teaching/Learning Process

The majority of the benchmarks regarding the teaching/learning process were considered both important and present on the campus. However,the benchmarks related to collaboration and modular learning were not endorsed widely. Benchmarks 22 and 23 were not seen to be very important and, likewise, did not display as high of a degree of presence at the institutions as other benchmarks in this category. Several comments may help to explain this. In general, faculty and administrators suggested that collaboration as an end in itself was not necessary.

Collaboration depends upon factors such as the content of the course, the level of instruction (undergraduate versus graduate), and the values of the instructor. Regardless of its importance, however, one faculty member noted that online students are collaborating much more than students in traditional classes.

With respect to modular learning, several respondents did not consider these benchmarks very relevant. Benchmarks 18 and 19 are, as one faculty member wrote, "...naive and passe. In several respects, we have gone beyond that."

Another stated that modular learning is not supported by the research and is not appropriate as a stand-alone benchmark.

Interactivity: Interactivity is the *sine qua non* for quality in distance learning. Indeed, many would say that it is crucial for *any* type of learning. As Otto Peters, author of *Learning* and Teaching in Distance Education, writes:

> If we take distance education seriously and understand it to be something more than the mere distribution and reading of study materials, we must provide sufficient opportunities for dialogues. If, in addition, we understand academic studies as a process in which the aim is education through *knowledge*, we cannot do without a considerable proportion of dialogical learning and teaching in distance education.

Many respondents agreed. One faculty member wrote that "Students need to communicate almost on a daily basis, not just once a week." Another noted that "in order to facilitate interactivity, in addition to e-mail and voicemail, a conference system is very important." One student reflected the observations of several others in stating, "The majority of online classes I have taken have been set up very well for a successful educational experience. The instructors for these classes encouraged communication between their students and themselves and were available to answer questions at any time through e-mail. They also provided timely and valuable feedback on assignments, which is very important for a student's academic success."

The notion of interactivity is highlighted here, not only because it is central to the quality of distance learning, but also because it leads to the realization that Internetbased distance education is evolving its *own* pedagogy.

As noted by the League for Innovation in the Community College and others, online courses have certain characteristics that are unique to the technology—which allows the exploration of new pedagogical models. Faculty are still learning about, and experimenting with, different ways that students can interact with faculty, other students, and a wide variety of instructional resources. One institution combines the use of asychronous technologies to facilitate much of the classroom interactions and synchronous communication to facilitate small group interactions and course office hours. With respect to interactivity, one faculty member lamented that, "Too often we try to emulate the classroom. Even software vendors try to emulate the classroom. The fact is that online learning is affecting how we teach in traditional classrooms."

Course Structure

In general, the course structure benchmarks were seen as both important and present at the institutions. However, benchmarks 25 and 26 addressing specific time requirements were the exception, scoring lower in terms of presence. Many respondents balked at the prescriptive nature of these benchmarks. Given the dynamic and innovative characteristics of Internetbased distance education, particularly the capacity for students to pace themselves in a variety of ways, hard and fast rules on how much work should be accomplished in a specific time period or the precise response time for a faculty member is inappropriate. One student responded to a minimum amount of time per week for study: "Yeah, they (faculty) give us recommendations, but they don't 'push' you.That's good! I enrolled in a [online] course so I would have the freedom to study at my pace and when I wanted to study. I did everything at my own pace for the first course and I got an 'A.' Therefore, stressing a strict pace is 'not important.'" However, there was strong consensus that faculty and students must agree when assignments need to be completed and returned.

The very high ratings for the benchmark regarding library resources are worth noting. In many respects, the library has come to the student's home or workplace. At several institutions, the librarian scans any article the faculty member requests, providing the full text online. In addition, the library resources include many online full-text books and, if needed, interlibrary loans. Reference assistance to students is not neglected and some respondents suggested that a reference person should be available 24 hours a day, 7 days a week. At least one institution required students to take a four-hour, non-credit course about library resources.

It may be helpful to examine briefly the issue of class size, although there are no benchmarks directly related to maximum class size. Because the case study revealed a wide variety of opinions, it is inappropriate that a specific benchmark on maximum class size be introduced. More than one respondent suggested that there should be a maximum size, say 20 or 25 students. Another recommended that the *first* online course a faculty member teaches should enroll no more than 15 students. Yet another institution is experimenting with class size and is incrementally increasing student enrollment in Internet courses. At the other extreme, one institution offers a two-credit orientation course with over 300 students enrolled.

When asked how much of the faculty time per week was required for the large enrollment course, the answer was about 20 hours. The instructor noted that appropriate interaction and successful student outcomes can be achieved in courses with large enrollments using a variety of methods, including student collaboration. It could be argued that maximum class size relates more to faculty course workload than student outcomes. It appears, therefore, that a specific benchmark for class size is ill advised, and much more experimentation needs to be conducted.

Student Support

Each of the benchmarks in this category were ranked as having a high degree of importance. However, it appears that, for at least three benchmarks concerning technical assistance and training for students, the institutions feel they have some way to go.

It is important to understand that traditional oncampus students are among those participating in Internet-based distance education, taking one or two online courses because it is convenient or to avoid conflicts with another course. Therefore, student support services provide for a broader audience than would otherwise be expected. Furthermore, it was noted that those students who are at a distance and do not come to the campus may have greater need for feedback than the traditional student. As one student noted, "I find that online advisement and school services other than course work is the real problem." To address this problem, one institution has established an electronic peer network in a web-based environment that enables students to interact academically and socially online. Students are able to identify other students with common interests, participate in live chats and threaded discussion groups, exchange books and study materials, locate study partners, access career resources, and/or join an online study group.

Many respondents recognized that a number of students need more preparation for working on the Internet. As a consequence, institutions provide technical help through a variety of ways, including an 800 number, e-mail, a real-time chat room, and an online tutorial for technical assistance.

Technical staff meet several times a year to improve the technical support based on student complaints. In areas other than technical assistance, student support personnel are devising several ways to help online students. One institution has set the goal of "one-stop shopping." To accomplish this goal, advisors have information on a computer screen that covers virtually all of a particular student's needs, including financial aid, academic program, tuition and fees, etc. At another institution, an advisor saw herself as a "coach," providing both support and encouragement for online students. These issues led several respondents to suggest that a new benchmark needs to be included under student support: "Questions directed to student service personnel must be answered accurately and quickly."

Faculty Support

With the possible exception of the benchmark addressing written resources for faculty on student use of electronically-accessed data, the rest of the benchmarks were considered very important. However, the three benchmarks concerning training and technical assistance for faculty had lower scores for presence.

Every institution in the case study has systematic processes for transitioning faculty to online instruction from the traditional classroom and for training and assisting faculty teaching online courses. Given that a substantial number of faculty teaching online courses volunteered for the assignment, and many are veteran teachers respected by their peers, their standards are quite high and their dedication is keen.

Information from the interviews strongly suggested that a major reason for the less than optimum presence of assistance was lack of resources, not lack of will. As noted earlier, several of the campuses are trying to keep up with student demand, while sufficient personnel and financial resources may be lagging behind. This is particularly true in the area of technical assistance. One faculty member lamented that the technical aspect of online teaching is sometimes overwhelming. Another faculty member wrote that "pedagogy of online learning must be part of training and the online environment."

Evaluation and Assessment

All of the benchmarks in this category are considered important by the institutions in the case study. Benchmark 43 addressing specific standards, however, had a relatively low mark for presence. By and large, all of the institutions had systems in place that addressed evaluation and assessment. More than one institution had elaborate evaluation and assessment procedures. It is clear that all of the institutions recognize the importance of evaluation and assessment.

One interesting evaluation system for online instruction that is still evolving invokes a medical analogy in which a physician examines a patient's vital signs to determine the patient's current state of health. Vital signs that are below acceptable standards are examined in more detail, utilizing more precise information and investigative techniques. In distance education, data are used to calculate a program's "health" rating in six areas: student demand: student retention; student satisfaction; faculty satisfaction; student achievement; and financial efficiency.

One issue that was mentioned by more than one respondent had to do more with outcomes, specifically student attrition. In The Institute for Higher Education Policy's 1999 report, *What's the* Difference? A Review of Contemporary Research on the Effectiveness of Distance Learning in Higher Education, concern regarding the apparent high attrition of online students as compared to traditional students was highlighted. One administrator mentioned that there seems to be an inordinately high number of the following grades:

"A," "F," and/or "W" (withdraw) for online students. Respondents from other institutions in the case study also referred to this problem. This anecdotal evidence suggests that there may be a bipolar distribution where students are either quite successful or dropping out. This further supports the conclusion in *What's the Difference?* that student attrition in Internet-based distance education courses is an important research topic in the evaluation and assessment programs of institutions.

Recommendations of the Case Study

The case study of six higher education institutions revealed that, for the most part, the benchmarks for quality Internet-based distance education were considered important and, in general, the institutions strove to incorporate them into their policies, practices, and procedures. At the same time, there were several benchmarks that did not enjoy consensus among the administrators, faculty, and students at the institutions and, in some instances, were not considered mandatory to ensure quality distance education.

The purpose of the case study is to help policymakers make judgments with regard to quality Internet-based distance education. The challenge, then, is to identify those benchmarks that are essential for quality distance education, in contrast to those benchmarks that contribute to and support the teaching/learning process, but are not necessary or required to ensure quality.

Analysis of the quality indicators at these institutions suggests that the benchmarks that are mandatory are those for which the absence of the benchmark would detract *from quality.* Stated positively, the benchmark must be essential or imperative to ensure quality in Internetbased distance education. Our recommendations are based upon the quantitative data from the surveys but are moderated by the hours of interviews with faculty, administrators, and students. Even though a particular benchmark may have received a high score for either presence and importance, the interviews informed and tempered our understanding.

The Institute's analysis of the data and information from the interviews resulted in the elimination of 13 benchmarks and the addition of 3 benchmarks. Moreover, several benchmarks were combined because they addressed the same issue(s) and were related to each other. The final outcome is a list of 24 benchmarks that are essential to ensure quality in Internet-based distance education.

Benchmarks That Are Not Essential:

The following benchmarks are not essential for ensuring quality Internet-based distance education.

— *Institutional Support Benchmarks*

— Faculty are provided professional incentives for innovative practices to encourage development of distance learning courses.

— There are institutional rewards for the effective teaching of distance learning courses.

This recommendation may be the most controversial. Both of these benchmarks enjoyed consensus with regard to their importance to ensuring quality. Yet, despite their relatively low presence at the institution, quality Internet-based distance education was occurring at every one of these institutions. The faculty involved in distance education were dedicated, experienced, enthusiastic, and exhibited a high degree of professionalism. Although they preferred to receive professional incentives and institutional rewards, the vast majority of the faculty engaged in distance learning because they were excited about it, they found it intrinsically rewarding, and they were already recognized by their peers as good teachers. Innovative distance education is happening every day without this benchmark. Moreover, many interviewees noted that distance education should be treated no differently than traditional classroom-based teaching.

— *Course Development Benchmarks*

— During course development the various learning styles of students are considered.

— Assessment instruments are used to ascertain the specific learning styles of students, which then determine the type of course deliver.

— Courses are designed with a consistent structure, easily discernable to students of varying learning styles.

The benchmarks addressing student learning styles received a cool reception from many faculty and administrators. In the view of several respondents, benchmarks addressing student learning styles were often platitudes with little basis in research and were very difficult to accomplish. While there is an implicit recognition of how students learn and an explicit understanding of the importance of interaction, constructive feedback, and other characteristics of good pedagogy, benchmarks that required these practices are not necessary to ensure quality.

— Course design is managed by teams comprised of faculty, content experts, instructional designers, technical experts, and evaluation personnel.

This benchmark was considered by many to be overkill. By and large, Internet-based distance education is the responsibility of the instructor and the academic department. The course development practices varied from department to department and institution to institution. The degree to which teams were formed for course design depended upon many factors, including the experience and knowledge of the faculty member, the degree to which the instructor asked for assistance, and departmental policies.

— Distance learning course development must be approved through a broad peer review process .

The majority of faculty and administrators objected strongly to this benchmark, particularly expressing concern about the definition of "broad." Peer review for distance education courses should be no different than that for traditional campus-based courses was a common refrain. In addition to concerns about academic freedom, subjecting distance learning courses to procedures that are more rigorous than the usual campus policies suggested a degree of oversight that was both unnecessary and detrimental to the ability of faculty to be innovative and responsive to student needs.

— *Teaching/Learning Benchmarks*

- — Courses are designed to require students to work in groups utilizing problem-solving activities in order to develop topic understanding.
- — Course materials promote collaboration among students.

The benchmark addressing the importance of collaboration was not viewed as essential to quality Internet-based distance education. It is important to note that many courses incorporated collaboration among students and some instructors even required it. However, including this benchmark as màndatory to ensure quality in distance education was not supported by a large number of interviewees. The decision to design collaboration in a specific course should be based upon several factors, including the difficulty of the content, course level, subject matter, and maturity of the students.

- — Courses are separated into self-contained segments (modules) that can be used to assess student mastery before moving forward in the course or program.

— The modules/segments are of varying lengths determined by the complexity of learning outcomes.

Similar to the arguments about collaboration, many faculty and administrators did not view modular learning as a requirement for quality. A few faculty, however, insisted that modular learning is a vital pedagogical activity. Others were equally insistent that there are several reasons for not designing a course or other learning activities in self-contained segments, as knowledge was integrated *across* several courses. The weight of evidence suggested that requiring modular learning as a prerequisite for quality distance education is inappropriate.

— *Course Structure Benchmarks*

— Specific expectations are set for students with respect to a minimum amount of time per week for study and homework assignments.

— Faculty are required to grade and return all assignments within a certain time period.

Many faculty and administrators were concerned about the prescriptive nature of these benchmarks regarding time expectations for students and faculty. Internet-based distance education is complex, and the pedagogy is constantly evolving as faculty experiment with a variety of techniques.

Moreover, much of the learning process is self-paced, which argues against the imposition of rigid standards. However, there was strong agreement that students and instructors each must have clear expectations of their responsibilities which should be no different than for any course, irrespective of its delivery.

New Benchmarks

There were three quality benchmarks that were not included in the original 45 but were recommended by a large majority of faculty and administrators and are consistent with the outlined criteria.

— The reliability of the technology delivery system is as failsafe as possible.

At every one of the institutions in the case study, a benchmark related to the importance of the reliability of technology was suggested. As stated by many, system crashes were unacceptable and must be avoided at all costs. When the system is down, essentially little to no learning takes place. If the system is down for any length of time, students often become discouraged, angry, and begin to lose interest. Even if the system is down for a short period of time, the experience is disruptive to students and fosters skepticism that it will happen again. Several faculty and administrators noted that student attrition is often related to system unreliability.

— Faculty and students agree upon expectations regarding times for student assignment completion and faculty response.

There are at least two benchmarks regarding faculty response to student assignments and feedback. There was strong agreement that faculty should respond to students as quickly as possible and that students need to spend a sufficient amount of time online to achieve academic success. The benchmarks were, however, too directive to be of much value. Many faculty and administrators recognized the potential of the Internet to transform the teaching/learning process and any benchmarks that inhibited their ability to innovate and experiment were rejected. This benchmark reinforces interaction and constructive faculty and student relationships without constraining pedagogical innovation.

— Questions directed to student service personnel are answered accurately and quickly.

Because online students may never have the opportunity to visit the campus from which they are taking courses or receiving their degree, it is essential that they enjoy the same access as traditional students to services such as admissions, registration, financial aid, career counseling, and academic course requirements. In fact, because they often do not have the opportunity for any face-to-face communication with student service personnel, extraordinary methods need to be developed to ensure that online students do not feel abandoned.

Benchmarks That Are Essential for Quality Internet-based Distance Education

The following represents the final list of benchmarks resulting from the study. These benchmarks are the most essential to the success of an Internet-based distance education program at any institution. These benchmarks may be useful to government policymakers, institutional decisionmakers, faculty, and students, as well as others with an interest in ensuring that the highest quality of higher education possible is being provided via Internet-based programs.

— *Institutional Support Benchmarks*

 — A documented technology plan that includes electronic security measures (i.e., password protection, encryption, back-up systems) is in place and operational to ensure both quality standards and the integrity and validity of information. : The reliability of the technology delivery system is as failsafe as possible.

— A centralized system provides support for building and maintaining the distance education infrastructure.

— *Course Development Benchmarks*

— Guidelines regarding minimum standards are used for course development, design, and delivery, while learning outcomes—not the availability of existing technology—determine the technology being used to deliver course content.

— Instructional materials are reviewed periodically to ensure they meet program standards.

— Courses are designed to require students to engage themselves in analysis, synthesis, and evaluation as part of their course and program requirements.

— *Teaching/Learning Benchmarks*

— Student interaction with faculty and other students is an essential characteristic and is facilitated through a variety of ways, including voice-mail and/or e-mail.

— Feedback to student assignments and questions is constructive and provided in a timely manner.

— Students are instructed in the proper methods of effective research, including assessment of the validity of resources.

— *Course Structure Benchmarks*

— Before starting an online program, students are advised about the program to determine (1) if they possess the self-motivation and commitment to learn at a distance and (2) if they have access to the minimal technology required by the course design. : Students are provided with supplemental course information that outlines course objectives, concepts, and ideas, and learning outcomes for each course are summarized in a clearly written, straightforward statement.

— Students have access to sufficient library resources that may include a "virtual library" accessible through the World Wide Web.

— Faculty and students agree upon expectations regarding times for student assignment completion and faculty response.

— *Student Support Benchmarks*

— Students receive information about programs, including admission requirements, tuition and fees, books and supplies, technical and proctoring requirements, and student support services.

— Students are provided with hands-on training and information to aid them in securing material through electronic databases, interlibrary loans, government archives, news services, and other sources.

— Throughout the duration of the course/program, students have access to technical assistance, including detailed instructions regarding the electronic media used, practice sessions prior to the beginning of the course, and convenient access to technical support staff.

  - — Questions directed to student service personnel are answered accurately and quickly, with a structured system in place to address student complaints.

- — *Faculty Support Benchmarks*

  - — Technical assistance in course development is available to faculty, who are encouraged to use it.

  - — Faculty members are assisted in the transition from classroom teaching to online instruction and are assessed during the process.

  - — Instructor training and assistance, including peer mentoring, continues through the progression of the online course.

  - — Faculty members are provided with written resources to deal with issues arising from student use of electronically-accessed data.

- — *Evaluation and Assessment Benchmarks*

  - — The program's educational effectiveness and teaching/ learning process is assessed through an evaluation process that uses several methods and applies specific standards.

  - — Data on enrollment, costs, and successful/ innovative uses of technology are used to evaluate program effectiveness.

  - — Intended learning outcomes are reviewed regularly to ensure clarity, utility, and appropriateness.

4

Web-based Teaching and Learning

The rapid expansion of the Web is moving educatinal systems to take greater advantage of the asynchronous modes of anywhere-anytime learning. It is widely believed that the web can be a powerful tool to enfranchise underserved learners via interactive learning and online support through a virtual community with a cultural sense of belonging. By gaining access to anywhere-anytime learning opportunities for completing a postsecondary education and getting workforce training, students will be prepared to make greater contributions in the knowledge society.

Higher education will need to take advantage of the broadband and high-speed access for online communication and learning that the telecommunications industry is deploying. New distribution systems to support Web-based education are being advanced combining the best of broadcast and narrowband. From Web-TVs to Internetenabled wireless devices, new delivery systems for Web content are being rapidly developed. The digital revolution will soon be flowing through broadband fiber optic lines moving an abundance of information never thought of before.

The explosion of broadband and wireless technologies is providing higher education institutions with extraordinary possibilities for assembling Web-based learning and reaching a wider and more diverse learner base anywhere-anytime. But it is a reality that the "digital divide" also exists among institutions of higher education.

Access is perhaps the most critical issue for making real the major potentials of Web-education. Major socio-economic and technological disparities exist in many regions, for example, among the Latino community geographically dispersed through the U.S. and Puerto Rico. The distribution of computers and the Internet is highly unequal across households and families.

As more services are processed electronically and more information is shared and communicated through the Internet, the need for computer literacy and the demand for online education and training, from anywhere and at flexible times, will be larger. Computers in public places such as schools and libraries, colleges, universities, and community-based organizations, will need to compensate for the low access that minorities have to personal computers and online services.

Producing online courses and exploring new models of teaching on the Web are moving simultaneously and a new class of teachers is evolving. Rather than mastering content as the prior focus of teaching, Web-based instructors or facilitators are learning to center on the learning experience. Faculty can now select among dozens of Webbased course management systems, such as WebCT, Learning Space, Course Info, and others, to design and organize their teaching strategies centered on the online learner.

But Web-education is not a technology. It is an emerging model of learning at a distance through a diversity of information and communication resources, and through mediated human interaction. Web-learning entails a knowledge-construction process resulting from the interactions of learners with instructors and other learners, through computer communication, and with distributed information resources accessible from anywhere through the Web's hypertext interconnections.

Careful instructional design with a constructivist view and assessment methodologies will insure the highest quality levels of online learning. Relan and Gillami define web-based instruction as: "...the application of a repertoire of cognitively oriented instructional strategies within a constructivist and collaborative learning environment, utilizing the attributes and resources of the World Wide Web."

Using constructivism in Web-based education entails the same principles used in a traditional classroom, such as higher level thinking, engaging students in a dialogue, encouraging reflective thought, independent learning and initiative, and using primary sources and interactive materials. Therefore, Web-based education should be characterized by the use of highly interactive communication and teaching strategies that engage learners in a virtual, dynamiclearning environment encouraging knowledge inquiry, research and critical thinking of Web-based and other resources.

Interactivity is considered a key aspect to successful asynchronous learning. Teaching strategies that best utilize the Internet are those that take full advantage of Web tools providing search capabilities, listserv, bulletin boards and structured chats for group discussions, multimedia and video streaming for concept visualization. These tools should be used to promote collaborative peer learning, give students more direct and convenient access to the instructor and other students, and make student contributions more formal, thoughtful, and precise.

Distributed resources and asynchronous communication through the Web have changed the definition of learning. Developing and encouraging the capacity to learn independently and collaboratively is crucial for all students, but particularly for minorities who are underrepresented in postsecondary education. A culturally sensitive, customized learning environment that can accommodate structured and interactive lessons with opportunities for collaboration, peer support and mentoring can be a particularly valuable holistic learning model for underserved learners.

Training and supporting the faculty for development of Web-based courses are crucial. Online educators need to be much more than regular Internet users. They need to be technologically literate in the management of multiple software programs to assemble information resources and learning strategies in a coherent and well-designed interactive course. They need to be innovative in their teaching paradigms and willing to redefine their role in Web-based education, and to explore, learn and utilize effective and interactive strategies for teaching online and assessing the learning experience. These skills will allow them to take full advantage of the numerous Web-based communication tools and course management systems to facilitate student interaction and active engagement in the construction of knowledge. Online teacher training has to be structured and continuous because

Web resources and tools are continually expanded and enhanced.

Faculty training and support for expanding Web-based education must be backed by institutional commitment. Faculty incentives, merit pay, release time, credit toward promotion and tenure, institutional recognition, and technical assistance are all motivating factors and support mechanisms for the growth of Web-based education. Higher education institutions will often have to decrease the academic load of some faculty in order to provide them with enough time to prepare for online course development and to compensate them when teaching online.

The Web can help provide learners access to more flexible education and training. Virtual learning environments will help provide wider access to education and training with greater flexibility. Nevertheless, embracing Web-based education should not be a survival tactic for higher education institutions, but a strategic path for transforming colleges and universities into new learning organizations building a new educational paradigm. Successful transformation requires redesigning learning strategies to create a new pedagogy. Developing Web-based alternatives in institutions will allow to open campus frontiers and expand academic offerings regionally and worldwide.

Experieces form Web-based Teaching and Learning

As a model for distance education WBL, *web based learning*, has become an increasingly popular concept and a common activity in many countries. This new medium offers many possibilities in approaching new groups of students. The opportunities to have students in several countries, and actually on several continents, in the same courses are promising and have many democratic advantages. However, there are several questions related to teaching and learning online and development of courses and course materials that we need to discuss, use and improve step by step.

At Malardalen University, the Department for Innovation Design and Product Development (IDP) currently offers four three-year programmes in Information Design. These programmes are called Text Design, Informative Illustration (Image Design), Expoand Event Design (Exposition Design). and Information Retrieval and Business Environment Analysis (Time Design).

After two years some students receive a university certificate (80 credits). Most students continue for a third year and become Bachelor of Arts in information design (120 credits). A few students continue to the master level (140 credits). A doctorate requires 160 credits additional to the BA, built up from a course segment comprising 80 credits and a thesis segment comprising 80 credits.

Currently there are some 300 students in the basic programs, 30 students in the master level and 3 doctoral candidates. The department offer a total of 70 academic courses. However, a large number of people have expressed interest in separate courses in information design. For various reasons it may not be possible for them to enter a total program. Some of them have a major in other disciplines and live in other parts of Sweden or even in other countries and working in a number of different occupations. For all these persons "distance education" and "web-based learning" may be an interesting opportunity. Therefore IDP started to develop a few experimental WBL-courses.

The course "Introduction to Information Design" provides basic knowledge of methods and theory for the designing of information materials. This knowledge is useful to information providers as well as information receivers. It is a "five credit course". This means that it will last for five weeks "full time" or ten weeks "part time". The student is expected to study for a total of two hundred (clock) hours. This includes lectures, seminars and work with assignments and time to read the required literature.

Since 1998 IDP offered the course "Introduction to Information Design" as a traditional course four times with a total of more than 300 students. Since 2000 IDP have offered the course five times as a distance course with about 100 students. In one course IDP had students both from Sweden as well as from the USA. "Information Design Overview" is a course on master level. So far the course has been offered once, with 36 students from different places in Sweden.

The department have used asynchronous as well as synchronous communication. Students had access to course literature and the assignments on the course web pages. They worked in study groups with their various assignments. To some extent the students searched for information on the Internet. They discussed the assignments and wrote their papers in collaborative and interactive work, sending drafts back and forth.

Some groups used e-mail, some groups used chatrooms, some groups used an electronic bulletin board, and some groups were actually able to meet each other face to face at different places. Students posted their reports asynchronously on the course web pages, for everyone to read when they had the time. In each course teachers had several synchronous chat-seminars with discussions on reports. They used e-mail for communication with individual students and with study-groups. They also used a bulletin board for messages, and techers acted as e-moderators during the synchronous chat-seminars and discussions.

Roxanne Hiltz is a pioneer in the promotion of what she calls "Asynchronous Learning Networks". Several of her studies indicate that collaborative learning at a distance may give as good results as classroom learning or even better. As to students' experience of their learning, Hiltz found that students experienced that they had a better access to their teacher. However, there is counterevidence to this finding. In one study, students felt neglected by the teacher and in another students found that teacher access was insufficient . The main difference seems to lie in the fact that teachers in Hiltz's research spent more time answering students' questions on-line. It seems that the interaction with the teacher is very important.

In another article Hilz focuses on how technology should support learning communities: "Colleges and universities ought to be concerned not with how fast they can 'put their courses up on the Web', but with finding out how this technology can be used to build and sustain learning communities. This does have fiscal implications: using collaborative learning approaches requires relatively small classes or sections of courses, which need daily attention from a faculty member".

Avgerinou concluded that despite the fact that research on learning differences in online distance learning is still in its infancy, there is already a great deal of consensus regarding the following findings:

— Online instructional design should consider and plan according to learning differences in order to empower all learners to attain their potential

— Reflector, visual and field-independent seem to be the most favoured group of learners in online environments

— Computer-mediated instruction may not accommodate all learners equally

— Providing opportunities for people to learn the way they prefer produces significant gains

Further Avgerinou reported that experiments which directly compared online learning with conventional, face-to-face instruction "consistently show that students can learn via the web just as effectively, or in some cases more effectively, than students in the traditional classroom".

The design of learning materials should be coordinated with a theory of meaningful learning. Mayer et al. built such a theory from components of Wittrock's generative learning theory and Paivio's dual coding theory.

Another issue concerns the integration of words and visuals in learning materials and information materials. The role of visuals in learning is unpredictable. The content, the structure, the context, and the format of a visual influence the viewer's ability to perceive its message. It can be concluded that pictures can have a positive, a neutral or a negative effect on learning. IDP propose that a nuanced analysis of the relationship between text and images is necessary.

The Department for Innovation Design and Product Development have surveyed students involved in WBL in a course on Information Design. it analysed their comments and also used a focus group. Its focus was to elicit opinions from the students as to the appearance of the web interface. the structuring of the course and the relation to the teacher and other students. Moreover, it wanted to get their general views on web based learning.

Of the total students 40 have provided their views and opinions on different topics in an inquiry and later some of them were invited to interviews. IDP also considered a large number of anonymous comments. Surveys on students involved in WBL were followed by analyses of comments made at a meeting with a focus group.

The instructors or e-moderators are involved in "action-research". Based on their experiences they have changed the design of course interaction step by step. One example is the design of the chat-seminars. In one course there were 30 students in the first of five chat-seminars. The teachres changed the structure to employ three chat seminars each with only two study groups with four to five students. During the course IDP found that a mix of asynchronous and synchronous modes of communication worked better.

Another conclusion is that WBL does not seem to save any time for moderators and/or teachers. *Firstly*, the course has to be carefully structured. Obviously this applies to all courses, but in a web-based environment there is little chance to modify courses while they proceed. *Secondly*, dialogues using e-mails, BBS or chat rooms take a lot more time and effort than regular teaching. It seems to be essential that the students feel that they are attended to – both by the teachers and their fellow students. Every single message will take form in letters instead of spoken words. *Thirdly*, the web interface has to be "transparent" i.e. easy to understand and easy to use. This is however easier said than done.

Some recommendations from the students were to develop and improve the seminars since chating is not always the best way to learn. Teachers can easily forget common technique i.e. telephone-conferences. The teachres often talk about *flexible learning* – now is the time to combine this with *flexible teaching*.

When asked what particularly ought to consider when develop new web-courses most of the students (80%) said that the concept and the logical structure of a course are the most important elements.

It is of course a complex matter to separate the logical structure from the GUI, graphical user interface. However, in the study students expressed a number of opinions on interaction.

Meeting face to face are very important and should be used, if possible, in every course. It seems that web courses that have those meetings work well and the students interact more than they do in courses lacking such meetings. It takes a lot of time to find a good structure and good concepts and this is not only depending on the subject or the teacher. it is also a matter of how large the group is, and its heterogeneity, e.g. if it is full-time or part-time students.

Naturally, it is likely that individuals differ in their habits of retrieving information from the web. The survey asked the students what could be used beside the Internet. More than half of the group (62%) said that *they want* to have "face to face meetings". One fourth of the students (27%) suggested "telephone conference".

This theme was followed up in the focus group and lead to a discussion on how to combine studies with other matters–many of them work full-time and study part-time. Sometimes their main occupations may constrain their possibilities to follow a course with a firm design and scheduled meetings.

The course structure should therefore allow some spontaneity, but in distance courses there are few chances to modify the approach during the process. Thus some students had found it difficult to contribute to some of the group assignments. It had been too hard for them to find time for chat-meetings. These students wanted more emphasis on individual assignments and less emphasis on group assignments in a distance learning course. They remarked that this way it would be easier for them to organise their "personal study scheme". Most of the student had experienced problems in finding suitable dates and hours for meetings.

One especially interesting matter appeared when the srvey team asked if WBL had changed the students' approach to *learning and knowledge*. 52 % answered "yes".

This is of course a very complex issue and so far one can not say so much about what was changed and why, but it seems that one can observe several advantages in WBL concerning "inter-social" and "international" group formations. The number of participants (40 students) is too small to confer overall significance but the discussion in the focus group confirmed the data from the survey.

From the surveys and the discussion in the focus group it is clear that IDP need to expand a number of different possibilities for communications among the students. such as "asynchronous web meetings". Finally, it was found that students expect to be advised and to be directed, but not forced to act in any certain way.

The context is just as important as in any other case, so consequently, the primary benefits of WBL are not economical (for the school) but concern the opportunity that new groups of students may be reached, i.e. those who would not consider go to university otherwise. Such students who may not be academically "literate" need a different approach.

In the study it was found that:

1. WBL does not save any time for moderators and/or teachers. It took a lot of time to find a good structure and good concepts.
2. Dialogues using e-mails, BBS or chat rooms take a lot more time than regular teaching. Every single message will take form in letters instead of spoken words.
3. It seems to be essential that the students feel that they are attended to – both by the teachers and their fellow students.
4. The web interface has to be "transparent", i.e. easy to understand and easy to use.
5. A mix of asynchronous and synchronous modes of communication worked better than any single mode.
6. Most of the students said that the concept and the logical structure of a course are the most important aspects to them.
7. More than half of the students said that they want to have "face-to-face-meetings".

8. WBL had changed the approach to learning and knowledge for 50% of the students.
9. Students expected to be advised and to be directed, but not forced to act in any certain way.
10. The primary benefits of WBL are not economical (for the school) but concern the opportunity that new groups of students may be reached, i.e. those who would not consider go to university otherwise.

Student Distress in Web-based Education

At least five different types of literature cover Internet-enabled distance education, including specialized research literature; practitioner literature, whose audience is administrators and faculty; instructional materials for students taking specific courses; popular accounts of such courses written for the public; and marketing descriptions of courses and degree programs. Most of this diverse literature emphasizes the likely value of Internet-enabled distance education for reaching new students, generating new revenues, increasing convenience, and possibly enriching educational experiences.

Some of the specialty research studies have examined the difficulties faced by instructors in developing and teaching these courses, or the problems reported by the students taking them. However, the majority of practitioner and popular articles tend to emphasize the virtues of distance education. Such articles frequently minimize the difficulties involved in providing high-quality distance education courses or in having students learn from them.

A study was conducted in US intented to increase understanding of the social process in such courses and of students' actual experiences in an Internetenabled course. The study article discussed a qualitative case study of a small, graduate-level, Web-based distance education course at a major US university. The study team used vivid ethnographic data, which included three methodologies: observation of relevant activities, such as classroom discussions, students' interactions with the course Web site, and a "field trip" to a virtual university; interviews and informal conversations with students and the instructor; and document review, including the course syllabus and reading assignments. They did not rely exclusively on electronic postings such as e-mail. For example, the study team interviewed and observed one student in her home when she participated in a "virtual field trip." Comparison of the information collected from the various sources helped to validate the data. The multiple data sources allowed for an increased understanding of students' actual experiences with and emotional reactions to the course.

Although some prior studies have cited isolation as a major problem in distance education classes, the study team did not find this to be of much concern to the students in the course. However, the recurrent experience of other types of distress, such as frustration, anxiety, and confusion, seemed pervasive. Further, the level of student distress the study teamfound in their study significantly exceeded their expectations.

From the interviews and observations, the study team found two foci of student distress: technological problems and communications. Students without access to technical support were especially frustrated, but the instructor's practices in managing her communications with students also produced stress in students. Students reported confusion, anxiety, and frustration due to the perceived lack of prompt or clear feedback from the instructor, and from ambiguous instructions on the course Web site and in e-mail messages from the instructor. The instructor did not appreciate the duration or extent of the students' distress, believing that she had effectively eliminated their anxieties and frustrations earlier in the term. Part of the reason for the instructor's misconception resulted from the students' reluctance to express their continuing distress to the instructor. The power differential between students and instructors in university courses probably influenced their relative silence. The study teamalso suspect that these difficulties were exacerbated by the weaker social cues found in asynchronous, text-based communication compared to face-to-face communications. Participants have to communicate overtly to create social presence online, whereas silent students' facial expressions and body language can communicate feelings in a face-to-face class.

Based on their results, the study team caution against emphasizing only the virtues of computer-mediated distance education, as is done in most articles written for practitioners and the public. In some of the earlier upbeat studies, students may not have had opportunities to express their confusion and anxiety with Webbased distance education. Data collected solely from course evaluations or students' e-mail might be skewed, as students might make more positive statements about the courses because of the relief of finishing the courses and concerns about upsetting the instructor. Thus, the study team recommend that future research on the topic of students' experiences of distance education use a multi-source methodology similar to the one employed here.

Methods of Effective Teacher Training

Today the new information and communication technologies have been used for the educatimg teachers. extension agents. health workers and other educational intermediaries including literacy workers. These methods make it possible to apply leverage to the solution of educational problems by strengthening the capacity of these intermediaries who play a key role in implementing government initiatives and as innovators of practice.Teachers' education presents formidable challenges to governments and other agencies. To be effective and to keep up with the demands made upon them. they require quality training on a recurrent basis. However, as the single largest category of public-sector employees, their pay alone accounts for the majority of the recurrent educational budget.

Teacher education has problems of quantity and quality. In quantity, the supply of teachers and teacher education has often lagged behind the expansion of schooling. In Africa and South Asia, millions more teachers are needed. Andrews et al. suggested that up to half the practising teachers in the developing world were unqualified in terms of their own country's formal standards for teachers' education: primary or junior-secondary school graduates are still being recruited to teach with no formal training. In such contexts, the traditional pre-service and in-service distinction is inappropriate; more useful is the distinction between initial training and continuing professional education. Problems of teacher supply and training are compounded by shortages in certain areas: specialist junior-secondary teachers, particularly in science and mathematics; rurally based teachers living in cultures or communities that restrict mobility, women teachers and male teachers at primary-level schools in western Europe and the English-speaking Caribbean. It is useful to distinguish between two different strategies for teacher education: providing formal courses, often for qualifications, and making resources available for teachers, but without the framework of a formal course. Both strategies have been widely used. Although we look at them separately below, they are increasingly interwoven to create richer, more flexible and multi-channel learning opportunities for teachers.

Course-based teacher Trainging

Most course-based distance education is aimed directly at teachers rather than at teacher educators. This has the advantage of bringing education more rapidly to the teacher than is possible through a cascade approach. In wealthy countries, communication technology is increasingly being employed within print-led teacher distance education for a variety of purposes: on-line teaching, networking, course delivery, assignment delivery and marking. We are also beginning to see more on-line courses. In Iceland, the University College of Iceland is offering on-line teacher education courses through The Icelandic Education Network. TRENDS (Training educators through networks and distributed systems) is a collaboration between seven European Union countries which aims to develop an in-service, schools-based teacher-training system using multimedia and network technologies. In Denmark, some teacher education is conducted via computer-mediated conferencing, satellite-based teleconferencing, multi-media and computer-based training. The British Open University is remodelling a course leading to a postgraduate certificate in education so that it involves extensive online teaching and gives entrants to the teaching profession an opportunity to use computer conferencing for interaction with other trainee teachers.

The use of interactive video technology – sometimes referred to as two-way audio, one-way video or interactive narrowcasting – has been used extensively in the United States but is a recent development in teacher education in some developing countries. This teleconferencing network approach has been employed to address the difficulties of training remotely located teachers and as an alternative to a cascade approach. In India, for example, the Indira Gandhi National Open University and the Indian Space Research Organisation initiated a seven-day pilot training course for primary school teachers in twenty different district training institutes in Karnataka State in 1996 as part of a broader Special Orientation for Primary Teachers programme.

In all, 850 teachers and 60 locally based facilitators at 20 district centres took part in the project. Studio-based educators made live one-way video presentations about different teaching areas – aided by prerecorded video-clips – to groups of teachers in the different sites. These teachers engaged in the particular subject area both before and after the telecast through print materials and activities produced centrally by the twenty-strong course team but mediated at the local level by trained facilitators. Direct questions to the educators could be made from the teachers through telephone and fax links. The approach used satellite transmission of the one-way video and two-way audio interaction, the production of video-clips, computer systems, cable television, telephones, and radio and television broadcasts.

During the seven-day course thirteen thematic areas were explored, covered in either morning or afternoon sessions. These included areas such as techniques for multigrade teaching, using the blackboard effectively, physical education, developing mathematics competencies and language teaching. Achievement tests, designed as part of the project evaluation, showed gains in competencies. An international project, operating mainly in Latin America, has been piloted by UNESCO and the Iberoamerican Association of Educational Television for environmental education. It involves co-production between ninety-eight different institutions in six Spanish-speaking countries – Argentina, Chile, Colombia, Honduras, Mexico and Spain. Eight universities from six of the countries each produced video programmes and print materials that present the variety of experiences in the field of environmental education - teaching methodologies, innovative teaching and use of technologies – but firmly embedded in the specific sociocultural contexts of each institution or country.

The project includes two steps designed to ensure interactivity. First, the videos are viewed and discussed by an interest group within each participating institution. The target audience consists of students of education, teachers and others interested in the topic. An expert in environmental education guides the discussion enhanced by written material, explaining the theoretical background of the proposal. Second, an international discussion on the proposal will take place. In the phase of this discussion the questions and suggestions which arose during the local discussion will be sent to the producers of the program. Then, each institution will be connected via e-mail to four other members, forming a sub-group of five. Within this group, each participant will have the opportunity to exchange ideas and experience with colleagues in other countries. An evaluation of the project is being prepared. If successful the model will demonstrate a way of achieving the necessary scale to justify the use of television while retaining some interactivity.

Most distance education for teachers, whether pre-service or in-service, is carried out through correspondence lessons 'seizing the advantages of a medium which could reach students anywhere – though some students more quickly than others – and could give them a text on which to rely' . In both industrialized and developing countries the print materials have sometimes been supported by radio and television broadcasts (often with cassette versions) and by tutorial support. Within industrialized countries there is an increasing use of computer technology used for additional on-line teaching, learning, networking, course delivery, assignment delivery and marking. In developing countries interactive technologies have played a minor role so far although this may change as the infrastructure of a country develops.

Particular combinations of media are often dictated by infrastructural and geographical realities. In Nepal, for example, the Radio Education Teacher Training Project used radio as the main medium for reaching primary-school teacher trainees because the mountainous terrain and lack of reliable transportation system made delivery of printed materials problematic. In the South Pacific and West Indies, audio-conferencing is used to facilitate discussion between teacher and tutors on different islands over large distances. In China, the massive scale of teacher education requirements resulted in television- and radio-led training, offered through the China Central Radio and Television University among other institutions.

The providers of distance education for teachers vary in organizational structure: dedicated large-scale open universities; mainstream universities with distance education units; dedicated distance teacher education colleges (National Teachers' Institute in Nigeria); and one-off, time-limited projects for primary teachers such as the Mubende Integrated Teacher Education Project in Ugandaand the Malawi Special Teacher Education Programme.

Distance-education programmes have been run for various deferent purposes. Some focus on initial training for unqualified teachers delivered either pre-service or in-service. Others provide further professional development to up-grade experienced teacher. Some give teachers an updating in new curriculum while others offer retraining in specific subject areas.

The Southern African Commonwealth Accord in 1998 was an agreement between several universities to pool and co-develop in-service training teachers in science, mathematics and technology subjects. Some distance education is aimed at teacher trainers.

In 1992, the Network for Teacher Upgrading, in Lao People's Democratic Republic, for example, started training 10 primary teacher educators in each of 8 regional centres by means of mixed-mode delivery – a combination of distance education modules and residential courses – in order to train 3,200 untrained primary teachers in remote areas by 1996. We have considerable evidence on the methodology, costs and effects of distance education for teacher training. Many distance-education programmes have achieved high success rates, or successful completion rates. In particular, where teacher-education programmes led to a qualification that increased a trainee's status and pay, motivation helped towards success. There is some evidence of changes in classroom practice as a consequence of distance-education programmes.

The main difficulty in executing programmes has been to organize classroom practice as an integral part of the programme and to supervise this practice. In some cases this has been made the responsibility of the staff of regular teachers' colleges. Occasionally in-school mentors have been trained to provide classroom guidance to trainee teachers. And, where the main aim of a programme has been to strengthen teachers' general education, a deliberate decision has been made to concentrate on these other aspects and not to monitor classroom practice.

Resource-based teacher Training

Alongside formal courses of teacher education, there has been a growth in programmes to provide resources for teachers and self-access learning opportunities for them. Information and communication technologies are being increasingly used for these purposes. They have two potential benefits. They can make educational resources of all kinds more readily available and can serve as a challenge of communication among teachers. In doing so, they can help overcome the isolation faced by some teachers and by teachers' colleges. A variety of innovative communication-based projects have demonstrated some of the potential. A number of projects have sought to use communication technology to create virtual communities of teachers, in the form of Internet interest-group sites or e-mail connected-networks of teachers.

There have been national and international moves to link teachers' colleges through information and communication technology. These projects assume that teachers are key agents for stimulating educational reform and that improved communications can help teachers initiate change within the education system from the grassroots level. Potential benefits are seen to include facilitating dialogue between practising teachers and college staff members, educational planners and policy-makers on issues related to learning and teaching. Some experimental projects of this kind have been launched within developing countries.

The United Nations has a set of Harnessing Information Technology for Development initiatives which includes a project on Creating Learning Networks for African Teachers project. It is intended to equip a maximum of four teacher-education colleges in each of twenty African countries with a computer and full access to the Internet in order to develop local, national and regional networks. The project, in its pilot stage, will also fund teacher education curriculum development in the area of mathematics and science, and the creation of twenty national educational websites.

In the pilot project in Zimbabwe, the participating colleges have developed their own websites, linked by a collaborative web-based platform, and all lecturers and trainee teachers have undergone an in-house computer literacy course. The project has had mixed results. While the percentage of computer literate lecturers increased to nearly 75 per cent, many lecturers found that, to use the system effectively, they needed more training than had been anticipated. Lecturers did not always feel confident in their use of computers and felt uncomfortable demonstrating to students.

At the same time, as access to the Internet was available from only one computer, practical constraints tended to be demotivating. Colleges are now considering networking computers within the college and increasing the number of computers with Internet connectivity. Lack of funding has limited the follow-up to this pilot project in Zimbabwe but other projects have started elsewhere in Africa. In Mozambique, for example, The WorldLinks for Development aims to connect all secondary, technical and teacher-training colleges to the Internet. Underpinning the project are computer literacy training workshops and pedagogical training modules extended first to a cadre of teacher educators and eventually to every teacher within each institution.The evidence seems to suggest that there should be significant practical benefits in using advanced communication technologies within teachers' colleges but that the practical problems of doing so, and of integrating them with the curriculum, are far from being overcome.

A range of non-formal organizations is also driving the development of virtual communities for teachers, especially in industrialized countries. Independent professional associations for teachers are increasingly on-line. TeacherNetUK, for example, aims to support teachers' professional development by selecting appropriate existing web projects, facilitating links to national and international teacher networks and developing on-line discussion groups for debate, dissemination of information and news.

Teachers can develop an online profile of their interests, needs and achievements, and then TeacherNetUK attempts to match the individual with accredited professional development programmes. Similar websites exist in many industrialized countries around the world. In Africa, the website Forum for African Women Educationalists posts articles on gender issues in education for children and teachers, has 'Networks for change' and is developing links to 'chapters' in all individual African countries.Other types of virtual dialogue for teachers are on-line experts and mentors. Teacher-learners can seek information and advice from organizations that offer ask-an-expert about particular subject areas, e.g. health and weather topics. Mentoring schemes offer one-to-one guidance to individual teachers by well-established members of the teaching community.

In an effort to increase the retention of new teachers, the United States National Science Teachers Association is providing first-year primary-school teachers with experienced teachers as mentors. In Australia, the faculty of education at the University of Wollongong is linking teachers directly to lecturers through e-mail networks and provides online support to teachers in school.

Mighty Mentors allows mentors and those they are advising to search for each other based on the levels at which they are teaching, their subject interest and their location. There is rapid growth in on-line teacher education resources mostly in North America, Australasia and western Europe.

These are as yet thin on the ground in developing countries, but their future development may help to redress the imbalance between the information rich and the information poor, and generate home-grown, culturally appropriate website resources. Resources vary from small-scale websites with downloadable materials in particular subject areas to larger-scale CyberLibraries consisting of a broad range of subject-oriented resources with state-of-the-art literature about integrating technology and good practice guidelines, curriculum resources and projects, links to lesson plans and classroom activities. Examples of the former include NASA's Classroom of the Future Program which provides teachers with literature about mathematics, science and technology education. Examples of the latter include TTS Internet Links and resources for Primary Teachers; the Teaneck Public Schools CyberLibrary, K–12 world CyberLibrary.

The use of CD-ROMs provides an alternative way of distributing information for those who have computers but no Internet access. Given the necessary agreement on intellectual property, CD-ROM distribution can provide access to educational literature which is not otherwise accessible to many teacher educators. UNESCO, for example, has developed Education CD-ROMs, available in three languages, each with the equivalent of 20,000 printed pages of teacher-education articles and references.

Low-tech approaches have also been followed in offering resources to teachers. In order to develop better English language skills among teachers, the national Self-access Project for Teachers' Colleges in Malaysia aimed to establish self-access English language learning materials – mainly print materials, audio-cassettes and some videos – in all twenty-eight teachers' colleges in Malaysia. This included developing resource centre management in addition to learner induction and monitoring. Self-access materials development projects such as these seem likely to become a growth area in the future and underpin the trend towards the development of decentralized community resource centres, used by a variety of target groups, including teachers.

In richer countries, well-established library systems often provide both the community resource centre and some teacher education opportunities. For example, the Herefordshire schools library service, like other libraries in the national library service of the United Kingdom, offers an INSET programme designed to enhance the teachers' or school librarians' existing library skills and to keep staff up-to-date with new resources – books, audio-cassettes, videos and CD-ROMs – that reflect national priorities in education and the national curriculum.

Educational broadcasting for teacher education exists but is thin on the ground. One example is that of Bombay Television Center which telecasts a 20-minute programme for primary-school teachers every week aimed at improving knowledge and skills. National television in India also broadcasts 45-minute programmes – Hints for Teachers – once a week during school hours on Saturdays in different languages to raise awareness about innovations in teaching.

Web-based Training (WBT) for Teachers

To many educators, web-based training (WBT) is the constructivist idealñ learners can construct meaning through self-directed inquiry, guided activity, and group collaboration on the information highway, the digital library, cyberspace, the global village. But is this vision of WBT as the constructivist ideal real or illusory.

Although experts may disagree on technical issues, WBT can include almost any kind of training provided through a network of computers (Driscoll 1999). Web computer-based training (CBT) is similar to CBT delivered via CD-ROM. In electronic performance support systems (EPSSs), online job aids and tools provide information to help workers solve specific problems.

Virtual asynchronous classrooms link users online at different times with communication tools like e-mail, online forums, bulletin boards, and listservs. In virtual synchronous classrooms, all users are online at the same time usingaudioconferencing, videoconferencing, chat rooms, and shared applications.

Constructivism, a theory of learning, holds that learners actively construct meaning by interacting with their environment and incorporating new information into their existing knowledge. Interaction and cooperationñkey elementsñallow motivation, support, modeling, and coaching.

Constructivist theory has important implications for both learning and teaching. Activities should be active, self-directed, learner centered, and collaborative. Information should be available in a variety of media and sequences to accommodate differences in modality, cognitive styles, and multiple intelligences. The instructor becomes a guide, facilitator, and coach instead of a transmitter of knowledge.

The career and technical education literature shows scant research on the effectiveness of WBT as a vehicle for constructivist learning, but findings from other areas can be applied.

Full, rich information. The very nature of WBT provides access to an incredible amount and variety of information:

— Trainers can provide any information that can be captured in a computer fileñ theory, examples, exercises, and tools that learners can use.

— The Web itself has so much information that no one even knows how much there is, what there is, or how fast itís growing.

— Communication tools (e-mail, listservs, bulletin boards, newsgroups) allow learners to seek, contribute, exchange, discuss, and debate additional information (Kilby 1999).

Differences among learners. The technological capabilities built into WBT can make information available in different ways to suit different learners:

— Information can be presented in almost any modality or combination of modalitiesñtext, still graphics, animation, audio, or video.

— Multiple intelligences can be accommodated by a wide array of software, multimedia, and other technologies.

— In the nonlinear information landscape, learners can use hyperlinks to access information in a selfdirected sequence appropriate to their cognitive style.

Learning activities. The technology of WBT allows learning activities that foster construction of meaning:

— Communication tools allow interactive one-to-one or many-to-many exchanges of informationñthe building blocks of meaningñindependent of time and place.

— Those tools also allow learners to manage the learning environment, the group process, and their roles.

— Asynchronous communication can allow more time for thoughtful reflection

The instructor as guide, facilitator, and coach. The technology of WBT can help instructors make the change from Sage on the Stage to Guide on the Side:

— Communication tools allow instructors to provide ad hoc guidance, advice, coaching, and feedback as learners construct meaning.

— Instructors can use hyperlinks, image maps, and threaded conferencing themes to provide scaffolding to guide learners in constructing meaning.

— Multimedia technology can engage learners and enliven learning through small group discussions, role-playing, learner presentations, brainstorming, simulationsñall online.

Although the technology of WBT allows, enables, and promotes constructivist learning, WBT does not always deliver in practice:

— Some learners need new technology skills before they can begin constructing meaning.

— Some instructors have difficulty incorporating WBT technology into their teaching.

— Some instructors find it difficult to be the Guide on the Side.

— Not all learners have the goals, interests, navigational skills, metacognitive skills, and prior knowledge of subject matter necessary to learn effectively in WBT.

— High-quality, interactive, multimedia, and nonlinear but scaffolded material is expensive.

— The sheer magnitude of the Web can magnify problems

found in any information systemñdisorientation, navigation, and information overload.

— Information on the Web may be unreliable, out of date, chaotic, or unavailable; technology can be slow and balky.

— Many websites contain nothing but unadorned textñno rich, nonlinear information landscape; no interactivity; no multimedia; no hyperlinks.

— The constructivist capabilities of WBT can be wasted in areas where memorization and rote learning may in fact be more appropriate.

Considering advantages and disadvantages, strengths and shortcomings, capabilities and cautions, we can draw some conclusions:

— Enormous amounts of information can be available on the Web and in custom WBT training materials.

— However, available information is not always accessible. Learners may lack the search skills necessary to find it.

— Available information is not always usable. Learners may lack scaffolding to connect it to their knowledge, group and communication skills to process it, or metacognitive skills to construct meaning with it; and the information itself may be of little value.

— The Webís versatile mix of software, media, and technology has all the capability needed for the interaction and collaboration among learners, their environment, and their instructors that constructing meaning requires.

— The capability for interaction and collaboration is not always used. Learners can encounter screen after screen of text without a single nonlinear hyperlink or alternative multimedia presentation; conferencing can go on and on with a single organizing thread as scaffolding; one-to-one, one-to-many, and many-tomany communication may be used only rarely or ineffectively.

— The built-in potential and capabilities of WBT for constructivism are not always appropriate for every learning task. Sometimes it may be more appropriate to transmit knowledge than to have learners construct meaning.

— The Guide on the Side is more than just a catchy phraseñitís a role that instructors must actually play, from the first step in planning to the final step in execution, in order to realize the potential of WBT for constructivist learning.

Clear implications emerge for policy and practice:

— Sound instructional design should drive the use of WBTñnot the appeal of technology for its own sake. Learning tasks should require constructing meaning rather than transmitting knowledge.

Implications

— Instructional planning should identify and provide appropriate scaffolding, advance organizers, hyperlinks, and multimedia for constructing meaning.

— Learners should receive training necessary to make effective use of any technology involved in WBT.

— Instructors should receive appropriate information and guidance to ensure that they act as the Guide on the Side, not the Sage on the Stage.

InterLabs innovative Web-lecturing tool

The InterLabs innovative Web-lecturing tool was designed and developed at Bradley University.It contains multiple features and functions of the above mentioned Web-lecturing tools. However, the InterLabs tool also offers the additional, attractive (for both students and faculty) features such as:

1) multiple "student-to-student' and "student-to-teacher" communication functions such as "call an audio-conferencing", "call a video-conferencing". "call a data-conferencing", "send an email", "join a discussion group", etc., and

2) control functions to download entire course and/or a set of modules of a course from the Internet (e.g., the Interlabs Server).

Today, the InterLabs tool can be used in three different modes on Web-lecturing, particularly:

1) "talking head" mode that is suitable for teaching classes in sociology, psychology, history, business, etc.,

2) "white board" mode that is suitable for teaching classes in mathematics, physics, chemistry, etc., and

3) "computer screen" mode that is suitable for teaching of computer science and information technology classes.

The distinctive feature of the INTERLABS tool is that it may be used in both synchronous and asynchronous modes:

1) in online mode (via a Web server) it uses the Microsoft Windows Media Player Active X control, Microsoft PowerPoint Player, Java Script, frames, Microsoft NetMeeting SDK, and several other tools, and

2) in offline mode (via a CD ROM) it uses the Microsoft Windows Media Player Active X control, Microsoft Visual Basic, and other tools.

In online mode, the InterLabs tool generates course content in the following modes:

1) PowerPoint slides only,

2) PowerPoint slides that are synchronized with streaming audio (for 56K modems),

3) PowerPoint slides that are synchronized with streaming video and audio (for 56K modems),

4) PowerPoint slides that are synchronized with streaming video and audio (for DSL and cable modems).

The InterLabs tool is also based on multi-agent technology. The agent technology has a great potential to assist on construction of virtual learning spaces that may include various pedagogic models, teaching and learning technologies and methodologies, forms of knowledge, collaboration and communication technologies, individual and team-working evaluation and assessment technologies of students/learners that are separated "in space and time".

The fundamental concept of InterLabs WBI tool is that it truly supports the active learning paradigm of education. The traditional approaches of learning have been questioned recently about their ability to provide the learner with "rich" rather than "minimalist" environments and with "authentic" learning experiences. Active learning became a modern paradigm of learning. It is a process rather than a product.

Active utilization of the InterLabs tool by students of several institutions clearly proves that it strengthens the advantages of active learning, specifically

1) student responsibility and initiative to promote ownership of learning and transferable skills,
2) intentional learning strategies, explicit methods of learning, reflection of learning processes, metacognitive skills,
3) goal-driven problem solving tasks and projects generating learning products of value,
4) teachers as facilitators, coaches and guides, not sources of knowledge, that requires discussion between teachers and learners,
5) authentic contexts for learning, anchored in real-world problems,
6) authentic assessment strategies to evaluate real-world skills, and
7) cooperative learning.

InterLabs tool and web-basd education theories

The learning theories that are applicable to the online education based on active utilization of the InterLabs Web-lecturing tool inclde:

1) Theory of Criterion Referenced Instruction,
2) Theory of Symbol Systems,

3) Adult Learning Theory,
4) Theory of Andragogy,
5) Experimental Theory,
6) Social Development Theory.

The InterLabs tool have been examined on integrative work with several approaches based on aforementioned theories. The preliminary results look very prospective. For example, it clearly demonstrated that the Web-lecturing technology and WBI tools strengthen the main advantages of the Web-based education and virtual colleges/universities for students such as:

1) convenience,
2) affordability,
3) accessibility,
4) total control over course,
5) lower cost of training (up to 25% - 75% over classroom-based education (CBE),
6) decreased learning time (up to 20% - 80% over CBE) and faster completion of education,
7) better learning gains/learner's understanding, and
8) higher retention factor.

More than 79% of Bradley students prefer the Web-lecturing technology rather than traditional "text -and-slides"-based WBI tools. Among the main reasons of their preference the students mentioned the following ones:

1) some parts and fragments of academic courseware are by far easier to demonstrate on a computer monitor than

to describe in textual format and series of images (using, for example, PowerPoint slides): therefore, those fragments can be understood better by students:

2) many students and adult learners reported that they prefer to watch video than read textual information.

Student-centered Model of Learning

Web-lecturing technology truly supports student-centered model of learning and personalizes learning process of each student. Particularly, it supports the following basic principles of student-centered learning:

1) Student Personal Learning Technology (student discover and construct knowledge using their personal learning technology from available information, personal perception, personal experience, available and affordable environment, thoughts and feelings):

2) Individualism of Students (not all students are at the same stage of physical, intellectual, emotional, and social development);

3) Student Creativity and Motivation (student are most creative when they are well-motivated and when learning is challenging and meets their individual needs and wishes);

4) Student Individual Past Experience (personal beliefs and impressions from earlier learning experiences color students' worldviews and their approaches to learning):

5) Friendly and Comfortable Learning Environment(students learn best in a friendly, comfortable, socially interactive, and diverse environment):

6) Student Limit of Perception and Learning (students tend to get tired of lengthy classes in different ways and conditions);

7) Student Personality and Curiosity (students have different degrees of self-confidence and they differ in the clarity of their personal goals and expectations for success and failure; additionally, students have different levels of curiosity).

Efficacy of Web-based Teaching Methods

A growing number of institutions have been implementing web-based, interactive experiments into their existing courses in a variety of subjects. For example, a web-accessible, virtual laboratory was implemented for an introductory-level engineering class at Johns Hopkins University as a solution to an over-registered class. Java applets were used to illustrate scientific phenomena and pose real-world engineering questions. This approach has also been used to teach abstract concepts in structural analysis at National Chiao Tung University.

A written test conducted before and after the virtual journey showed that the students acquired basic knowledge of structural analysis from the exercise. Comprehension and application of structural analysis, in addition to basic knowledge, were also tested. The literature indicates that there are unique teaching advantages associated with an interactive web-based teaching approach. Web-based assignments allow for additional perspectives not possible in a laboratory setting, allow the learner to proceed through an experience during a broad time period not fixed by a regular class schedule, and makes learning more interesting. Lastly, an interactive simulation of an environmental engineering design project was shown to be an effective way to supplement theory-based course content without increasing student loads or placing excessive time demands on the instructors. This section explains the significance of an interactive web-based thermodynamics assignment

The undergraduate thermodynamics course in the Mechanical and Aerospace Engineering Department at San Jose State University is a 4-unit lecture course with no concurrent laboratory course. It is a required course for Mechanical and Aerospace Engineering majors. There are typically between 60 and 80 students enrolled per semester. The following are some of the factors that prompted the development of the interactive web-based assignment:

A. *The need to illustrate theory.* Because thermodynamics is an abstract subject with many non-intuitive concepts, it is less intimidating and easier to understand when real-world applications of the theory are provided. Traditional problem sets of hypothetical engineering scenarios are often assigned for this purpose. However, a large percentage of engineering students are visual, sensing, and active learners and it is necessary for them to see and experiment with things before they can fully understand engineering concepts. An interactive illustration of a physical thermodynamics experiment on a computer screen could fulfill this purpose. The operation of the experiment could be shown with photographs and videos, and a graphical interface could be developed to provide a self-guided virtual tour through the assignment.

B. *The need to serve a commuter campus.* Because most of our students live and work off-campus. the convenience of a web-based assignment is of great benefit. A web-based assignment can be accessed anytime from any location with Internet access, unlike a physical laboratory experiment or a problem session. In comparison, the logistics involved in scheduling laboratory sessions to demonstrate an experiment for a large class are often prohibitive.

C. *The need to accomplish more with less in a crowded curriculm.* Our degree programs are faced with a number of conflicting demands such as a large number of required general education courses, political and societal pressures to help students graduate in four years, and the need to modernize the curriculum to reflect the latest technological advances. The web-based approach offers a way to introduce visual and experimental teaching tools into existing courses without increasing time demands on the instructors or students.

D. *The need to incorporate modern teaching tools.* Because the Internet is a way of life today that was unimagined even ten years ago, most college students are proficient at navigating and finding information on the web. On-line engineering assignments leverage this trend as they connect textbook theory with a convenient source of information should the desire to do further research develop.

E. *Safety and cost considerations.* Other considerations include the safety and low cost of the web-based assignment. The dangers associated with boiling, condensing and combusting substances often used in thermodynamics experiments are eliminated with a computer simulation. Lastly, costs such as facilities, technician support, maintenance, supplies, and student laboratory assistants are not required for this type of approach.

The use of web-based experiments has the potential to reinforce the learning of an abstract subject matter more effectively than the traditional approach of lecturing and assigning problem sets. While it will never duplicate the "hands-on" aspects of a physical laboratory experiment, it could offer many of the same benefits and has its own unique advantages from a teaching perspective.

To determine the most effective way to incorporate this approach into an existing course, a web-based thermodynamics assignment was developed based on an existing steam turbine experiment and introduced into the undergraduate thermodynamics course at San Jose State University. The learning objectives were assessed through an assessment survey, performance on the assignment, and student feedback. By determining which learning objectives were most effectively accomplished with this approach, conclusions on the most suitable use of this teaching tool can be determined for the development and use of future web-based assignments.

The scope of the web-based steam turbine assignment encompasses the following goals and learning objectives:

— *Goal 1*. Reinforce theory through steam turbine analysis. The learning objectives for accomplishing this goal include: using thermodynamic charts to obtain steam properties, performing mass and energy balances on steady-flow components, and calculating isentropic efficiency. Students are then expected to reflect upon the calculated results to obtain a general understanding of how to measure and influence the power output of a steam turbine.

— *Goal 2*. Provide real-world examples of components and sensors. In lecture, steam turbines and sensors are presented only as schematics. Interactive photographs and videos, although they do not replace actual hands-on experience in the laboratory, bring students closer to the actual hardware. Goal 3. Provide training in experimental uncertainty. Textbook problems usually have a preferred methodology and a unique right answer, unlike real-world problems that are often subject to measurement uncertainties and non-ideal conditions. Students need to appreciate the engineering judgment needed to account for such factors.

The design of the web-based assignment considered the motivation for this project and the type of interactive features that would accomplish the learning objectives. In addition, the information gained from the prior literature about the teaching efficacy of various virtual reality techniques was considered. There is an abundance of software tools available to implement interesting interactive web sites. It was decided to use HTML and Javascript to implement interactive photographs and Quicktime Pro to implement a virtual reality movie of the apparatus.

The interactive photographs were designed to address the goal of providing real-world examples of components and sensors described in lecture. Steam is routed first through a turbine and then through a heat exchanger cooled with water. A dynamometer is used to measure steam turbine performance. As the mouse is rolled over components and sensors in the schematic, the corresponding part in the photograph is highlighted. This serves to identify parts, explain how components are connected, and show where the sensors are located. A rotatable apparatus was implemented to further address this goal. It was implemented using the Quicktime Pro Virtual Reality module. In this feature, the user can click and drag a photograph of the apparatus to rotate it as if he or she were walking around it. In addition, the user can zoom in or out of any particular view. Furthermore, select views are labeled if there are components of particular importance or interest.

Sources of experimental uncertainty were reflected in the assignment by imitating the actual sensor outputs in the experiment. The fluctuating components of measurement uncertainty were recorded during data acquisition, and implemented in the web-based assignment using the random number generation feature in JavaScript. As a result, the webbased data vary slightly from one reading to the next, as they would in real life. Students then learn the value of averaging multiple samples to obtain a more representative measurement. In addition, the pressure sensor located at the inlet to the steam turbine exhibited a slight offset error that implied a subcooled liquid in one of the six required cases. The student is then called upon to re-examine the experimental setup and speculate why the readings appear to be inconsistent. The use of this kind of engineering judgment is lacking from traditional problem sets, which tend to make idealizations and assumptions to eliminate inconsistencies.

The data analysis required of the student focused on reinforcing the techniques of mass and energy balances.

determining phase and properties using steam tables, and calculating the isentropic efficiency of the turbine and its significance. The load and revolutions per minute (RPM) of the turbine are varied using the dynamometer, and the resulting torque and flow measurements are used in the calculations.

There were six cases total, each requiring the determination of the properties of superheated, saturated, and subcooled water, energy balances on the turbine and heat exchanger, and calculation of isentropic efficiency. Graphs of power output versus the input parameters were required, as well as a writeup of the experimental procedure and an analysis of the results.

Links to related web-sites such as steam property calculators, unit conversion calculators, animated steam engines, and history of steam power were bundled with the web-based assignment to spur further interest in the topic. Having the assignment on the Internet makes this route of obtaining further information seamless and fun.

The teaching efficacy and the appropriateness of the learning objectives for this type of assignment were assessed with the results of an assessment survey, performance of the students on the assignment, and anecdotal feedback. The web-based assignment was shown to be more effective at accomplishing the learning objectives in comparison to traditional problem sets.

During the spring semester of 2003, the undergraduate thermodynamics class at San Jose State University was given the choice of completing either the web-based steam turbine assignment or a problem set that covered the same lecture topics. Otherwise, the lectures, problem sessions and available office hours were identical. The lecture topics covered were: mass and energy balances on steady flow components such as turbines and heat exchangers, determining phase and properties using the steam tables, and calculating isentropic efficiencies for steady flow components. Of the students for which a full set of assessment data were collected, 33 chose to do the problem set, and 9 chose to do the web-based assignment. It is unclear why so many more students chose to do the problem set. It is speculated that the problem set was perceived to be the "easier" assignment.

The assessment survey tested concepts covered by the lecture topics as well as component identification and function. The survey was administered before and after the assignments to both groups. The questions and learning objective or goal tested are listed in Table 1. On each question, a score of 1 was given if correct, and 0 if incorrect.

Table 1. Assessment survey questions for web-based steam turbine assignment

No.	Question	Learning Objective/Goal
1	The power output from a turbine is proportional to: a)isentropic efficiency, b)torque, c)torque times RPM	Measuring and quantifying power output
2	Identify the following components: (photographs of a torque sensor, heat exchanger, and pressure gauge follow.)	Component identification
3	What does a dynamometer do?	Component identification
4	What does an isentropic efficiency of 90% mean?	Understanding isentropic

		efficiency
5	Which properties are sufficient to fix a state in the vapor dome? a)temperature and pressure, b)temperature, c)enthalpy and pressure, d)temperature and quality.	Using steam tables to find properties and phases

On the whole, both groups of students were roughly of comparable ability prior to the assignments. The group of students who chose to do the web-based assignment started out slightly stronger on Questions 1 (quantifying power output) and 2 (identifying components) and less strong on Question 4 (understanding isentropic efficiency) than the students who chose to do the problem set. The average scores on Question 3 (identifying components) and 5 (fixing steam states) were similar. There is no underlying pattern to the strengths and weakness of either group; therefore, it is concluded that the apparent advantage of the web-based assignment group is slight. However, it is clear that the web-based assignment was more effective at teaching the concepts tested by the assessment survey than the problem set.

Webbased assignment group improved on Questions 2 through 5 with perfect scores on Question 3. The problem set group improved less dramatically on Questions 2 and 4, and did worse on Questions 3 and 5. The fact that both groups did worse on Question 1 by a similar amount suggests that the timing of lecture topics with the administration of the assessment survey may have contributed to a misleading interpretation of that particular question. Both assignments were graded out of 100 points and counted for 15% of the final class grade. The average scores were 88% and 80% for the webbased assignment and the problem set groups, respectively. The goal of providing training in experimental uncertainty in real world applications was met by the web-based assignment, and not assessed in the problem set due to the nature of the two assignments. A discussion question on the web-based assignment asked the students to ponder sources of measurement uncertainty and resulted in answers such as sensor offsets, fluctuations in the experiment, variation in atmospheric conditions, and human error.

The web-based assignment seemed to be more enjoyable than the problem set based on anecdotal student feedback received through the website, by email, and informal discussions. In general, the comments from the web-based assignment group remarked how rewarding it was when the process diagrams and isentropic efficiency graphs in their textbook were duplicated with real-world data, despite the tediousness of the calculations. Both groups complained of the length of the assignments, although this subset of students was primarily composed of those that did not start the two-week assignment until the last minute.

The interactive web-based thermodynamics assignment is more effective at reinforcing theoretical concepts discussed in a lecture setting compared to a more traditional problem set. In addition, the valuable concept of experimental uncertainty is addressed with the web-based assignment unlike a traditional problem set. Because the time required by the instructor to administer and grade an assignment were similar for both, it is concluded that the web-based assignments are a more effective teaching tool for the type of learning objectives tested. Replacing problem sets with this type of assignment is justified by the added teaching efficacy and benefit to the students when the initial development time is available to the instructor.

5

World Wide Web — The Boost of Distance Education

In the last two years, a new technology has grown enormously in importance and accessibility. This technology, the World Wide Web, lends itself beautifully to constructivist, active learning. The World Wide Web is a part - the fastest growing part - of the internet. In 1989, a group of scientists at the European Laboratory for Particle Physics (CERN) in Geneva, Switzerland began developing an Internet tool that would link information produced by all of the CERN researchers. The tool provided a way to link textual information on different computers and created by different scientists. The object was to overcome issues of incompatibility and utilize a new way of linking made possible by computers, called "hypertext". Rather than presenting information in a linear or hierarchical fashion, hypertext permits information to be linked in a web-like structure.

The CERN project resulted in an innovative front-end to the Internet, now referred to as the World-Wide Web

(WWW). The WWW provides users with a uniform and convenient means of accessing the vast resources of the Internet. In 1993, the National Center for Supercomputing Applications (NCSA) at the University of Illinois pushed the CERN scientists' idea further by creating a software tool called Mosaic. Mosaic is an easy to use graphical user interface that permits text, graphics, sound and video to be hyperlinked. Mosaic was the first of the Internet tools that are now referred to as " Web browsers". Other well-known browsers include Netscape (the first commercial browser developed by some of the programmers involved with the Mosaic project) and Microsoft's Internet Explorer.

Web browsers permit users to connect to the Internet and facilitate accessing information located on another remote computer. The Web browser links to the remote computer just long enough so that the information you need can be sent to your computer for you to view. Documents created to be viewed by a browser are formatted using Hypertext Markup Language (HTML). HTML solves incompatibility problems by using standardized tags which indicate such things as whether a piece of text should be plain, bold, italic, or linked to another piece of text. Pages of information on a computer formatted with HTML and accessible to someone with a Web browser, are referred to as "home pages" or "Web pages".

The WWW and Web browsers have made the Internet a more user-friendly environment. The ability to integrate graphics, text, and sound into a single tool means that novice users do not have to struggle with such a steep learning curve. In addition, organizations and individuals can create home pages independently and link to other home pages on their own computers or to pages created by others on different computer systems. For educators, the WWW provides an exciting new opportunity for distance teaching and learning. The WWW can be used by the distance educator to build a classroom home page. The home page can cover information about the class including the syllabus, exercises, literature references, and instructor's biography. The instructor can also provide links to information on the WWW that would be useful to students in the class (e.g., research data on agricultural markets, global climate change, or space missions). Other links can access library catalogs or each student's individual home page. In addition, the home page can link students to a discussion list or listserv that set up for student communication. It is also a relatively simple matter to use the homepage to create forms that students can fill out and that will end up being sent to you as an e-mail message.

What makes the World Wide Web especially exciting is that it also allows you to create anchors that download files for you or allow you to send e-mail to an individual. The web thus makes it easy to gain access to data, software and people. It's a user-friendly front end to almost everything on the internet. Within a year or so, the mechanics of creating documents on the web will become transparent. Most publishers of word processing software are adding the capability of saving documents in web format to their ever-growing list of features. So far, however, the end result of using a word processor to create web pages directly may not be exactly what you had in mind. An active webwriter will want to know how to tweak the appearance of the documents and, for the moment, that requires some familiarity with HTML. HTML, or HyperText Markup Language, is easy to learn.

To prepare a page for the web, you just embed special characters or tags in your document to tell your browser how to display a given word. For a computer trainer, learning the basics of HTML should take no longer than a weekend. Excellent resources for learning HTML can be found on the web, and are indexed in A Primer for Creating Web Resources. The Web 66 Internet Server Cookbook contains recipes for putting pictures and sounds in your pages, serving downloadable files, and maintaining a server from a distance. An alternative method for displaying content on the web is the Adobe Acrobat format. This allows complex page layouts to be used, but users of your materials must all have the proper helper application installed on their machines. In a corporate environment with software standards in place, this shouldn't be a problem. Once you have created your pages, you simply upload them to the server you'll be using.

Most medium to large-sized corporations have already established a web presence, and many smaller companies have as well. Whether you purchase space on the machines of an internet provider or set up your own webserver, you need not be physically near the server itself. Most maintenance can be done from a distance. Once the use of the web as a way to distribute course materials is second nature to you, the next phase is to take advantage of all the material that's out there beyond the walls of your institution. The more you incorporate such activities into your course, the more it will become transformed into an learner-centered environment and the less often you'll find yourself holding forth on center stage. If you can get friends and colleagues, both in and outside of your enterprise, to volunteer to answer questions, you've broadened the pool of experience available to your students. Newsgroups provide an invisible college of people helping people. They are a great source of up to the minute news about software releases, bugs, and workarounds. If you have your own newsserver, you can also set up internal newsgroups specific to your course to provide a space for students to exchange information on an ongoing basis. Most newsgroups maintain a list of frequently asked questions that have come up within that group. These can be a rich source of materials and pointers to other resources on the web. Most major software publishers (e.g., Microsoft, Novell, Claris, Adobe) have placed their technical notes on the web.

Patches, applications, utilities, documentation... there are many sources of useful wares ready to be downloaded. FTPing (i.e., grabbing) and decompressing this software is handled transparently by your web browser. You can place an anchor on a page that refers to a file and all your users have to do is click on it to have it delivered to their desktop. Suppose you're teaching a course on desktop publishing and you want your students to have the experience of dealing with a difficult client. One way to bring that kind of encounter into the classroom is to set up an e-mail address with a fabricated name. Periodically, you answer the mail at that account while acting like someone else.

Distance educators who are ready to develop a web presence, should avoid the following pitfalls:

— *Rushing in without a master plan*: Don't get so caught up in learning HTML and developing the home page that the purpose for developing your presence on the WWW is lost. Spend less time struggling with HTML, developing amusing graphics or playing with possible background and more time considering the purpose and content of the home page.

- *Before you start your home page*: Think about your reason for developing a Web presence. Sound instructional design principles apply to home pages just as with any other materials prepared for a course. Become familiar with new software tools for developing home pages. Computer software tools such as HotMetal and HotDog mean that anyone familiar with using word processing software can develop a good looking and functional home page.

Utilize information that already has been developed for your course. If you already have your notes and syllabi in word processed form, make use of tools such as HotDog to format them for distribution on the WWW. Hundreds of home pages have already been developed for courses. Some of these home pages allow students to complete an entire course from the WWW and others are developed in conjunction with lectures delivered on-campus or by video or audio.

Utilizing a consistent format for each of your pages. Based on suggestions made by the above mentioned style manuals, develop a consistent format for each web page. While colored or patterned backgrounds can be used on homepages, plain grey or white backgrounds make text easier to read. Keeping page lengths short. Your main index should jump to a lot of shorter pages. In cases where page information is long, index internally so that the student can jump to specific information as needed. Maximizing links to internal information and minimizing links to external information. The purpose of your home page is to provide information on a specific subject area. Only provide external links to home pages that provide useful related information for your students.

The home page should help your students to find necessary course information, learn the material, and get involved in thinking about the course material. Properly designed home pages will encourage thought, discussion and active participation by your distant students. The following elements can be included in your class home page:

— *Course and Instructor Information* — Include such items as course topics to be covered, your office hours, textbook information, course objectives, and grading policies.

— *Class Communication* — Provide access to your e-mail, link to discussion groups that you have set up for student-to-student communication, and create forms that your students can use to report problems or provide biographical information about themselves.

— *Assignments and Tests* — Distribute assignments and tests, provide for online completion or submission, and give solutions, hints, or samples of what you expect.

— *Material covered in the classroom* — Make lecture notes and handouts available either as web pages or as downloadable files.

— *Demonstrations, Animation, Video, Audio* — This is more complex than other suggestions and will require that your students have access to computers with sound and video cards.

— *Reference Material* — List materials in print and electronic form that supplement the textbook. To avoid copyright problems, electronic articles should either be written by you or in the public domain (e.g., government documents or are already available on the WWW with author's permission to distribute). In addition, provide links to other pages which cover information on the topic, similar courses that may also be available on WWW, your university library, and other on-campus resources that may help your student complete the course.

For many people who are new to the web, the temptation to browse and pursue one link after another is so strong that they spend countless hours glued to the screen. In an educational or training situation, however, we don't have the luxury of spending all of our time that way. As much as we value curiosity and exploration, it's necessary for us to find ways to get the greatest learning benefit from the web in the shortest possible time. At San Diego State University we've been thinking about how to do that, and one lesson format that we've developed toward that goal is called a WebQuest. A WebQuest is an activity of guided inquiry in which learners are given a task which requires internet access to complete.

WebQuests can be designed as short- or long-term activities. At the end of a short term WebQuest, a learner will have grappled with a significant amount of new information and made sense of it. A short-term WebQuest is designed to be completed in one to three class periods. WebQuests are deliberately designed to make the best use of a learner's time. There is questionable educational benefit in having learners surf the net without a clear task in mind, and most educational and training institutions must ration student connect time severely.

To achieve that efficiency and clarity of purpose, WebQuests should contain at least the following parts:

— An introduction that sets the stage and provides some background information.

- — A task that is doable and interesting. The task could include a series of questions that must be answered, a summary to be created, a problem to be solved, a position to be formulated and defended, a creative work, or anything that requires the learners to process and transform the information they've gathered.
- — A set of information resources needed to complete the task. Many (though not necessarily all) of the resources are embedded in the WebQuest document itself as anchors pointing to information on the World Wide Web. Information sources might include web documents, experts available via e-mail or realtime conferencing, searchable databases on the net, and books and other documents physically available in the learner's setting.
- — A description of the process to follow to complete the WebQuest.
- — Some learning advice on how to organize the information acquired. This can take the form of guiding questions, or directions to complete organizational frameworks such as timelines, concept maps, or cause-and-effect diagrams.
- — A conclusion that summarizes what they will have accomplished or learned by completing this WebQuest.

It is a simple matter to place a form on the web that collects information from your learners. To actually send that information to the server and process it, though, goes beyond simple HTML into the realm of CGI: the Common Gateway Interface.

It is here that most web developers stop because creating CGI programs at this point requires the ability to program in C, Perl, or AppleScript. As time goes on there will be ready-made CGI's available to accomplish most tasks, but for the near term there's a learning curve here that stops most people.

Future of Net-Based Training

The net world is moving quickly towards greater interactivity and sensory engagement. There are several developments worth watching. Some websites allow you to click on a picture and hear a greeting or introduction in the form of a sound file. You have to wait for the file to download before hearing anything, though, which tries the patience of all but the most fervent websurfers. RealAudio is different. It begins to stream audio to your workstation almost immediately. It's like radio on demand. For distance education, the usefulness of RealAudio is obvious. All of the spoken communication that makes up a bulk of a traditional class can be digitized and made available as needed. As long as this doesn't lead back to the "talk, chalk and a hairy arm" tradition, RealAudio could become a standard feature of distance education on the web.

Virtual Reality Modelling Language is an embryonic set of tools and conventions for portraying three-dimensional space on the web. Instead of seeing a static picture, you'll be able to hold your mouse down over a graphic and see it from multiple perspectives, zooming in for detail and veering in any direction.

For distance education, this allows for a more intuitive depiction of content: imagine seeing bubbles labeled with all the major concepts in your course. Lines linking the bubbles represent the relationships among them. Zoom in on a bubble and you've arrived at a webpage describing it in more detail.

You might also use VRML to create a simulated learning environment with a reference room, laboratory, and help desk. Java is a language for writing small programs (applets) that are downloaded as part of a web page. This will allow the web to take on most of the characteristics of the interactive multimedia you would find on a CD-ROM.

MOO stands for Multi-user dimension, Object-Oriented, which doesn't at first convey much about its meaning. A MOO is a shared virtual space that people can help create from their own computers. You can set up your conference room the way you like it and invite others to join you there. At present, most MOOs are text-based. When they begin to become more graphical, (soon) they will become the most popular places to be in cyberspace. These developments, and others, will make distance education more and more practicable on the web as time goes on.

Web-based Distance Learning Tools

In recent years, colleges and universities have spent a great deal of time and effort in looking inward to analyze the efficacy of learning through the use of technology. This includes policy papers, "how to" articles, and essays, as well as a limited, though not insignificant body of original research. With few exceptions, the bulk of these writings suggests that the learning outcomes of students using technology at a distance are similar to the learning outcomes of students who participate in conventional classroom instruction. The attitudes and satisfaction of students using distance learning also are characterized as generally positive.

Because distance education is perceived as an increasingly effective method of instruction, educational researchers have examined the purposes and situations for which distance education is best suited. Research indicates that the instructional format itself has little effect on student achievement as long as the delivery technology is appropriate to the content being offered and all participants have access to the same technology.

Distance learning generally includes synchronous communication, which occurs when teacher and student are present at the same time during instruction-even if they are in two different places-and asynchronous communication, which occurs when students and teachers do not have person-to-person direct interaction at the same time or place.

Research suggests distant students bring basic characteristics to their learning experience which influence their success in coursework.

Good distance teaching practices are fundamentally identical to good traditional teaching practices and "those factors which influence good instruction may be generally universal across different environments and populations".

The Internet is the largest, most powerful computer network in the world. It encompasses 1.3 million computers with Internet addresses that are used by up to 30 million people in more than fifty countries. As more and more colleges, universities, schools, companies, and private citizens connect to the Internet either through affiliations with regional not-for-profit networks or by subscribing to information services provided by for-profit companies, more possibilities are opened for distance educators to overcome time and distance to reach students. With access to the Internet, distance educators and their students can use:

•

— *Electronic mail (e-mail)* - Like postal mail, e-mail is used to exchange messages or other information with people. Instead of being delivered by the postal service to a postal address, e-mail is delivered by Internet software through a computer network to a computer address.

— *Bulletin boards* - Many bulletin boards can be accessed through the Internet. Two common public bulletin boards on the Internet are USENET and LISTSERV. USENET is a collection of thousands of topically organized newsgroups, covering everything from supercomputer design to bungee cord jumping, and ranging in distribution from the whole world to single institutions. LISTSERV also provides discussion forums on a variety of topics broken out by topic or area of special interest.

— *World-Wide Web (WWW)* -The WWW is an exciting and innovative front-end to the Internet. Officially WWW is described as a "...wide-area hypermedia information retrieval initiative aiming to give universal access to a large universe of documents". The WWW provides Internet users with a uniform and convenient means of accessing the wide variety of resources (pictures, text, data, sound, video) available on the Internet. Popular software interfaces, such as Mosaic and Netscape, facilitate navigation and use of the WWW. The central organizing feature of the WWW is the "home page". Every organization and even every individual user of the WWW can create a home page that contains whatever information they want to present. The hypertext capabilities of the WWW facilitate linking of information within your own home page and with all other home pages on the WWW.

Distance educators can use the Internet and WWW to help students gain a basic understanding of how to navigate and take full advantage of the networked world into which they will be graduating. Some instructional possibilities of the Internet include:

— Using e-mail for informal one-to-one correspondence. Feedback from the instructor can be received more quickly than messages sent by mail. Students can read messages at their convenience and easily store them for later reference.

— Establishing a classroom bulletin board. Distant students often work in isolation without the assistance and support of fellow students. Setting up a class bulletin board can encourage student-to-student interaction. With a class computer conference, individual students can post their comments or questions to the class, and every other individual is free to respond. The conference can also be used to post all modifications to the class schedule or curriculum, assignments/tests, and answers to assignments/tests.

— Engaging students in dialogue with other students, faculty, and researchers by encouraging them to join a bulletin board(s) on topic(s) related to the class.

— Developing a classroom home page. The home page can cover information about the class including the syllabus, exercises, literature references, and the instructor's biography. The instructor can also provide links to information on the WWW that would be useful to students in the class (e.g., real research data on agricultural markets, global climate change, or space missions). Other links could access library catalogs or each student's individual home page.

When incorporating the Internet into a distance delivered course, remember that:

— All students in a course must have Internet and WWW access to ensure equal opportunities for computer interaction and feedback. Also, convenient access to a computer at home or work may influence student success.

— Students may face the concurrent challenges of learning basic computer skills, new software, and appropriate online communication skills. Trouble-shooting student computer problems will probably become a part of normal instructional responsibilities. Setting up a specific classroom conference for ongoing discussions of specific hardware and software problems may help students to work through these problems on their own.

— Some students might hesitate to contribute to computer conferences or to send e-mail because of a lack of familiarity with the proper protocols. Encourage students to use e-mail, classroom conferences, electronic bulletin boards, and the WWW early in the course so they overcome inhibitions. Specifying a minimum number of e-mail communications per week will encourage active participation.

— Using e-mail can help the instructor provide feedback more quickly than surface mail or telephone. Prompt response generally increases student motivation and performance.

— Prompt responses might not always be appropriate. Computer conferences can foster student-to-student interaction. To ensure that this interaction is sustained, work towards a facilitative role. It might be appropriate to delay response to a query in a classroom conference in order to allow students to respond to the issue and to each other.

— Becoming familiar with the resources available on the Internet and the most effective ways to use them will be part of the instructional challenge. A number of helpful guides to the Internet and WWW are available.

Expansion of Distance Education

Higher education is in the midst of a virtual revolution. In the 1980s, advances in microcomputing revolutionized academic data collection and analysis alike and gave rise to the Internet as a means for academic researchers to share data. In the 1990s, we saw the extraordinary growth of distance education (DE) in higher education, particularly Internet-based courses at the collegiate level. These include both credit and non-credit courses, even full degree programs, and the numbers continue to rise.

According to a report by International Data Corporation, in 2002 approximately 85 percent of two- and four-year colleges will offer distance education courses, up from 62 percent in 1998. For the same time period, student enrollments are projected to increase from just over 500,000 to well over two million students. What is causing this expansion? For one thing, college administrators often report that they are responding to the likelihood of large enrollment increases coupled with shrinking public budgets and, in particular, the disinclination of public officials to build new brick-and-mortar institutions. Another motivation is the desire to provide educational access to students who are unable, or find it extremely inconvenient, to attend a traditional institution.

Academic supporters of distance education are attracted to the challenge of providing quality education through a new medium. Some advocates maintain that student demand is an important reason for the growth of distance education, although there is mixed evidence on that point. Another likely factor in the growth of distance education is the general cultural shift toward digital communications.

Clearly, however, one critical component of the expansion of distance education is the perception that it offers the potential for making big money. According to the US Center for Education Statistics, education and training accounted for $700 billion a year in the American economy, with distance education grabbing an increasing slice of the education pie. The potential market for distance education seems to grow with each new estimate. According to one report, Merrill Lynch projected that the distance education market would reach $7 billion by 2003. A report by Thomas Wiesel Partners put the number at $10 billion in 2003, and another report by Merrill Lynch forecast the total "e-learning" market, including all education and training, at $25 billion by 2003.

Regardless of the real dollar value, in 1999, when Cisco Systems CEO John Chambers pronounced education "the next big killer application on the Internet," investment money poured in, with as much venture capital flowing into education that year—an astounding $6 billion—as was invested in the entire decade of the 1990s. Thus, a potential is seen, as Professor Dan Schiller maintains, for "the Net (to kick) the ongoing metamorphosis of education into overdrive."

Existing Institutions

Some college administrators explain their adoption of DE in terms of gaining access to new student populations. Others cite competitive pressure to maintain existing enrollments vis-a-vis for-profit distance education providers and other existing institutions. Among elite colleges, there is the desire to protect the quality of their "brand" name and still fall in line behind the DE bandwagon. At some institutions, DE initiatives are pitched as a way to keep faculty members from selling their courses to other vendors. In a recent highly publicized case, Harvard took steps to prevent one of its well-known law school faculty members, Arthur Miller, from selling a set of Internet lectures to the Concord University School of Law—an online law school.

One example of a university that has created a significant online program is the University of Illinois. Established in 1997, the University of Illinois Online currently enrolls students in 26 online programs, including one professional degree, 10 complete master's degrees, and a baccalaureate completion program. The U of I Online does not separately admit and register students; instead, it coordinates the university's online offerings and provides research and student services for online learning.

Similarly, the State University of New York (SUNY) Learning Network is another large DE consortium, offering graduate, undergraduate and non-credit courses from 53

SUNY campuses. Like Illinois Online, the SUNY Learning Network does not offer separate degrees; each degree comes from an individual SUNY campus. Faculty participation in the program is voluntary. Courses listed in the SUNY Learning Network catalog are approved through regular channels on each SUNY campus.

Rio Salado Community College offers one of the largest distance education programs at the community college level. One of 10 separate institutions in the huge (9,000-plus square miles) Maricopa Community College District in the greater Phoenix area, Rio Salado was founded in 1978 as a center for adult education. With no central campus, this self-described "college without boundaries" originally offered courses in high schools, libraries and community centers in the Phoenix area.

In 1996, Rio Salado began to add online programs to its extensive menu of distance learning courses and training programs. Today, Rio Salado delivers 80 percent of its general education courses via the Internet or other DE technologies. New course selections at Rio begin every two weeks and students can study at their own pace, which offers flexibility for working adults. Rio Salado employs 18 full-time faculty and 600 part-timers, and every faculty member is required to teach at least one online course.

The faculty role at Rio Salado is "unbundled," or broken down into a series of discrete tasks. Design teams—which include a technical trainer, an editor, a proofreader, and Web and content specialists—create a curriculum and standardized courses that are taught primarily by adjunct faculty.

Rio Salado College is one of a handful of U.S. institutions that participate in the Pew Learning and

Technology Program's Grant Program in Course Redesign. This program was based upon ideas found in the National Learning Infrastructure Initiative, in which modular, online exercises, tutorials and quizzes would replace more expensive direct contact with actual faculty in high enrollment introductory courses.

According to Carol Twigg, coordinator of the Pew program, such redesigned introductory courses should enhance the quality of education by individualizing the instruction, assessing students' learning more frequently and providing students with more specific feedback. The "primary goal" of the program is "to shift from a passive, note-taking role to an active learning orientation in order to enhance learning outcomes." The "significant cost savings" generated by the course redesign could then be used to reduce tuition, or be given to "faculty members involved in the redesign...as an incentive or a reward for increasing productivity." At Rio Salado, Introductory Algebra was select-ed for redesign, which had the third highest enrollment of the top 25 courses in the entire community college district. Course content was delivered via interactive software. The restructuring increased the student faculty ratio from 35 to 100 students per instructor, although each faculty member was assigned teaching assistants to help with technology questions and students had access to a help desk.

In a few cases, universities have created for-profit spinoffs for their distance education programs. One reason for the switch to for-profit status is access to capital. Recent estimates place the cost of infrastructure needed for colleges to offer online courses at $25 million. Moreover, even though many universities have attempted to limit the amount of money spent on distance education infrastructure and courses, some private, for-profit companies have spent at least $1 million to develop a single course. Thus, with colleges and universities embarking on a kind of educational arms race, some institutions have sought significant outside funding in order to launch new distance education programs.

The first for-profit online subsidiary was created in 1998 at New York University. The curriculum at NYU Online is marketed to corporate clients such as American Express and Morgan Stanley Dean Witter. At first, NYU contracted with Click2learn, a company that provides the technical expertise and software necessary for DE courses.

More recently, the institution has developed its own facilities for producing and marketing distance education. Some instructors at NYU Online are drawn from NYU's tenured faculty; others are adjuncts. Teaching is broken down into a series of discrete steps. One professor designs a course, instructional designers set up the course online, and another instructor teaches the course, in some cases, replying to students in real-time chat sessions.

When asked whether this process compromises faculty control over the curriculum, Ron Chalmers, NYU Online's director of academic operations, replied that it did not. There were, he said, some accommodations that faculty must make when using the DE medium. Their favorite 15-minute lecture, for example, could not be condensed into a text box in a DE template that was limited to 256 characters. In this case, faculty would have to improvise when converting traditional courses to distance education.

But Chalmers was quick to point out that faculty participation in NYU Online is voluntary and that when courses were developed for distance education, faculty were always the final authority. He argued further that new DE course software would allow professors—who have a basic knowledge of computers and half a day of training —to perform all the functions of a DE design team, thus making the disaggregation of the teaching functions unnecessary.

The first *public* university in the United States to create a for-profit DE spinoff is the University of Maryland, which established the University of Maryland University College online program in 1999. At UMUC, students worldwide have access to 24 complete bachelor's and master's degree programs. With an enrollment of 40,000, UMUC bills itself as the world's largest online university. UMUC was created with private sector investment, in part the result of a Maryland law, since repealed, that required distance education organizations to be self-supporting. In the last five years, however, UMUC has received approximately $40 million in state support.

Other for-profit spinoffs are still in the pipeline. Temple University has announced plans for a "Virtual Temple," and Cornell University trustees have approved a resolution for an "e-Cornell".To date, neither of these online programs has begun to offer courses; and both of these programs engendered considerable faculty opposition on their respective campuses. At Temple, the faculty senate passed several resolutions related to Virtual Temple. One requested that any course offered online be approved by the university's faculty senate—the same process used for on-campus courses. Art Hochner, president of the AFT local at Temple, noted that the faculty had a variety of concerns regarding Virtual Temple. One concern was a lack of faculty involvement; another was that Virtual Temple courses would be taught by "poorly paid part-timers" instead of full-time faculty members.

Corporate- University Joint Ventures

The second category of new distance education providers consists of corporate-university joint ventures. These hybrid partnerships can be further divided into two subcategories:

— Those that provide course management systems for colleges and universities to offer their own DE courses and programs, and

— Those that package and distribute courses or content from existing institutions.

Course management systems: When colleges choose to offer distance education, administrators must choose from several options. One is to develop their own hardware and software to offer DE in-house. Another option is to develop some of the capabilities for DE, which might include the software templates for DE courses, for example, while contracting out for the hardware and training necessary to host full-scale DE programs. A third option is to contract with outside vendors. This group of vendors is noteworthy because distance education is expanding most rapidly through existing institutions adding distance courses to the established curriculum. The outside vendors who provide hardware, and, most important, course management software, are consequently tapping the largest market. Web CT is the leader in this understandably lucrative market, which provides a variety of software, course tools and hosting solutions to more than 2,600 college and university clients. Web CT currently serves more students and faculty than the next largest vendor, Blackboard.

Blackboard is the fastest growing firm in this sector with more than 1,900 colleges and universities as clients, including such well-knowninstitutions as Johns Hopkins, Duke and the Ivy League schools. Blackboard has raised more than $50 million with backing from America Online, Dell Computer and Pearson Education. In December 2000, the U.S. Army announced that Blackboard had been selected for a $435 million DE program for soldiers.

Other vendors in this sector include Campus Pipeline, based in Salt Lake City, which provides campus Web platforms for more than 65 colleges and universities, and eCollege, which provides DE hosting capability on a number of campuses.The firm most likely to dominate this market will be the one that can successfully integrate DE course management with student information systems; this would allow students to register for courses, check their grades and attend DE classes —all from the same computer screen.

Likewise, faculty members could grade student papers, check their transcripts and track their enrollment, using the same computer interface. It is little wonder that one DE administrator described this as the "holy grail" for private course-management vendors.

In May 2000, Web CT took an important step toward reaching this goal. It joined with Campus Pipeline and SCT, a company that provides more than 1,000 higher education student information systems, to create an alliance that could "deliver a full range of administrative services, campus intranet offerings, distance learning resources, community tools and Internet content from a single login."

Package and distribution systems: The second category of corporate-university joint ventures comprises vendors that package and distribute courses or educational content from existing institutions. One of the most ambitious of these new DE joint ventures is Fathom, Columbia University's for-profit DE consortium. Fathom does not offer degrees or administer individual courses, but instead acts as a distribution channel for its 13 prestigious member institutions and other colleges and universities whose courses have been added more recently.

These include the University of Chicago, the Rand Corporation, the American Film Institute, the London School of Economics, the Smithsonian, the British Museum and the New York Public Library. Recently, Fathom has begun to list courses from the University of Washington, University of Florida, the University of Buffalo, Iowa State University and the University of Southern California School of Engineering among the 600 courses on its Web site.

Fathom markets itself as the source of highquality DE content. For quality control, Fathom relies on two separate groups. The first group, which includes faculty and administrators from Columbia University Teachers College, approves all courses offered on the Fathom Web site. In addition, an academic advisory council composed of one representative from each of the 13 member institutions oversees other educational content on the Web site. Ann Kirschner, Fathom's CEO, says the consortium currently is developing a number of short courses and seminars that fall between the two poles of individual lectures and semester-long courses. Fathom is also developing humanities courses, which is rare among the new, mostly business-oriented DE providers.

There is also a great deal of free content on the Fathom Web site, which Kirschner says, has two purposes. The first is to project the teaching and research mission of Fathom's member institutions. The second is to provide an entry point for people who are curious about distance education but not willing to sign up for a full semester course. The obvious question is whether Fathom can develop a market for high-end (and high-brow) intellectual content delivered via the Internet. According to the *Wall Street Journal*, Fathom has "about 75,000 registered users," while the number of students actually paying for online courses numbers "only in the hundreds."

According to a draft report by the Columbia University senate, Fathom has yet to make a profit. The report noted that Columbia recently was forced to commit $10 million—on top of its original investment of $20 million—to keep the consortium afloat. In the meantime, Fathom has postponed advertising and laid off staff. According to Kirschner, Fathom's lack of profitability reflects the fact that DE has yet to be fully integrated into higher education. Until that happens, she maintains, Fathom must work on adding more courses and "evangelizing" for distance education.

Cardean University: The online subsidiary of UNext.com, is a fully accredited, online, graduate business school. Backed by former junk bond king Michael Milken and Oracle CEO Larry Ellison, Cardean is affiliated with prestigious MBA programs at Columbia, Stanford, Carnegie Mellon and the London School of Economics. The University of Chicago, has an especially strong influence, John Gould, former dean of Chicago's business school is Cardean's president and Andrew Rosenfield, a professor at Chicago, is president of UNext.com.

A degree from Cardean, however, is separate from any of the affiliated institutions, which raises the question of whether business school students will flock to this less well-known (and not yet regionally accredited) "brand" name. Cardean is promoted as a high-quality, comprehensive program for business professionals, and most of its nearly 100 courses are marketed to companies for in-house training. Cardean is also very well funded. UNext reportedly spent $1 million developing the institution's first four courses and has committed $120 million for Cardean's first three years of operation. In case Cardean were to fold, UNext's Rosenfield reportedly offered each partner institution a guarantee of $20 million in exchange for their affiliation. But given Cardean's strong backing and institutional pedigree, many well known businesses have signed on. By the end of 2000, 14 major companies had signed up for Cardean to provide distance education to their employees, and more were in the pipeline.

Cardean's curriculum is based upon the idea of "problem-centered learning." Cardean students are presented with distance education simulations of crises they might confront in the corporate world. Beginning with specialized business courses in the summer of 1999, today Cardean offers a complete online MBA and a total menu of almost 100 courses. Masters courses, which require 25 to 30 hours, cost $500 each. Shorter quantum courses, each requiring two to three hours, are priced at five for $380. Teaching at Cardean is unbundled, with "senior" faculty planning the curriculum, "advisory" faculty counseling students and supervising adjuncts, and "adjunct" faculty members working with students by grading assignments, answering e-mail and directing online discussions.

Another ambitious online joint venture is Global Education Network (GEN), the product of an alliance between Williams College humanities professor Mark Taylor and investment banker Herbert Alan Jr. As with Fathom, GEN is one of the few for-profit DE providers committed to bringing the "soft" subjects of the humanities online.

GEN, in fact, plans to offer a full undergraduate core curriculum in a few years, with faculty drawn from small, prestigious liberal arts colleges, which are not usually associated with distance education. Not surprisingly, GEN markets itself as a high-quality DE access point; currently on the Web site are courses from individual faculty at Williams, Wellesley and Brown. The privately owned GEN reportedly has institutional relationships with Wellesley, Brown and Duke, although many other institutions—including Williams (Taylor's home campus) have chosen not to affiliate with GEN. The main objection at Williams was that associating with a DE provider would hurt its quality reputation. Other distance education joint ventures—some with significant outside funding—are attempting to capture the estimated $4 billion that corporations spend each year on DE training for their employees.

Founded in 1997, Cenquest offers business courses and graduate degree programs in partnership with a number of university MBA programs. Cenquest's original affiliates were the Oregon Graduate Institute of Science and Technology and the University of Texas at Austin. Working with these institutions, Cenquest adapts their courses for the DE market by dividing them into shorter units, which are then offered on a rolling schedule either for individual applications or degree and certificate programs such as accounting, which are more readily standardized and modularized. In December 2000, Cenquest affiliated with the prestigious Babson College to provide an MBA program to Intel employees. Cenquest has been successful in attracting venture capital. It began offering DE courses, which now number over 100, in 1998.

A similarly well-funded DE provider ($55 million) is Quisic, which is partnered with the London School of Economics, University of Southern California's Marshall School of Business, and Financial Times Knowledge, a business education provider. Formerly known as University Access, Quisic has moved beyond its original focus in the undergraduate DE market and today is primarily concerned with business education and training. Quisic has been aggressive in expanding its market of more than 200 corporate clients. Also organized for the overseas DE market is Universitas 21, a consortium of 18 institutions of higher education from around the world. Still in the planning stages, Universitas 21 is attempting to secure the participation of major U.S. institutions.

Virtual Universities

Moving further away from traditional university models, virtual universities make up the third category of new distance education providers. These are online institutions that typically operate without brick-and-mortar campuses. The current private operators of online universities enroll less than 5 percent of all students in postsecondary distance education, although this number is growing rapidly.

Perhaps the most successful—and one of the most controversial—of the new virtual institutions is the University of Phoenix Online. Founded in 1976 by CEO John G.

Sperling, Phoenix is the nation's fastest growing proprietary higher education institution. The North Central Association of Schools and Colleges (NCA) accredited Phoenix in 1978. From November 1999 to November 2000, Phoenix increased its overall enrollment (both on and off line) from 68,000 to 84,000 students.

Although the institution maintains 55 campuses and 98 learning centers in 18 states and abroad, it is best known for its rapidly growing DE component. Phoenix Online, as it is called, has pursued an aggressive growth strategy. Its tracking stock, issued by its parent company, the Apollo Group, raised $70 million from Wall Street investors on the first day it was offered. Phoenix Online's enrollment increased 67 percent in the past year, from 11,100 to 18,500 students.

Geared toward working adults, the University of Phoenix curriculum emphasizes vocational education and goals. Phoenix offers an associate of arts degree in general studies and an associate of arts degree through credit recognition, as well as bachelor's degrees in business-related subjects and graduate programs in business, management, health care management, nursing, education, counseling and computer information systems. In 1999, Phoenix began offering a doctor of management degree in organizational leadership.

As Phoenix's online catalog explains, its curriculum "...is designed in cooperation with the business, industry or profession to which the degree program relates." Classes are held on evenings and weekends to accommodate adult professionals. A typical undergraduate course at Phoenix lasts five weeks; graduate courses are six weeks. Students attend one four-hour "workshop" per week or meet for longer sessions on alternate weekends. Students also take classes sequentially—one at a time—so they can better focus on the subject matter while working full-time. An additional requirement is that students work in teams.

As Phoenix's online catalog explains, The university organizes each class into problem-solving teams of the type employed successfully in business and industry. Thus, in addition to the development of intellectual and technical knowledge, the student is able to grow emotionally so that the potential for practical application of knowledge and skill is optimized.26 An estimated 90 percent of Phoenix faculty (both online and classroom) teach part-time. At its Northern California brick-and-mortar campus, Phoenix employs 20 full-time faculty and 550 parttimers. These part-time "facilitators," as they are called, must possess a graduate degree from a regionally accredited institution and must work full-time in a field related to the courses they teach. They receive training from the university that, in the case of the online faculty, consists of six weeks of online training and five weeks of additional "special instruction and mentoring on how to teach online classes effectively."

Those with no teaching experience are paired with faculty mentors, who receive part of the new faculty member's salary. Phoenix's part-time "practitioner faculty," as they are also called, are not eligible for tenure or benefits, although they are reimbursed for expenses. The salary average is $1,200—ranging from $950 to $2,000 for an on-site course and from $900 to $1,280 for an online course. This depends on the level of the course and the training of the instructor; Phoenix claims that all instructors have full-time employment in the discipline in which they teach.

Phoenix faculty work in a highly structured environment. Course facilitators in traditional classes are forbidden to lecture. Faculty are, instead, expected to closely follow Phoenix's "teaching/ learning model," which begins with course syllabi and detailed teaching modules developed by full-time faculty on the main campus. In this way, faculty responsibilities are broken down into a series of discrete steps, such as when course development is detached from teaching. Phoenix course modules "include guidelines for weekly assignments, group activities and grading." Some course modules contain classroom time-management guidelines broken down into 15-minute intervals.

Phoenix defends its practice of using these restrictive guidelines in the name of standardization. The university's online catalog declares: "The standardized curriculum for each degree program provides students with specified levels of knowledge and skills regardless of the delivery method or classroom location."

Critics argue, however, that Phoenix's course modules violate academic freedom because they don't allow faculty members sufficient discretion. Milton R. Blood, managing director of the American Assembly of the Collegiate Schools of Business, has characterized Phoenix's standardized curriculum as "McEducation." He explained, "It's a redefinition of how we go about delivering higher education. The question is whether it's really higher education when it's delivered in a franchised way."

Located in Englewood, Colo., Jones International University is the nation's first fully accredited, exclusively online higher education institution. When JIU was accredited by North Central in March 1999, some 96 percent (54 out of 56) of its faculty members were hired on a parttime basis. JIU, a for-profit subsidiary of Jones International, which is a cable and media firm, uses an instructional model which draws upon many of the same practices found at the University of Phoenix.

Teaching at JIU, for example, is partitioned into discrete processes, such as course development and instruction. Administrators at Jones International, like Joe Gregg, director of content and product development, contract with faculty at outside institutions, who are known as "content experts," to create JIU's courses. The courses are taught by JIU's almost exclusively part-time "teaching faculty," who are paid $600 for a bachelor's-level course and $700 for a master's-level course.

Like Phoenix, the JIU curriculum is geared toward working adults. At the time it was accredited, JIU offered 36 courses and two degree programs (B.A. and M.A.) in business communication. In March 2000, Jones announced the creation of its fully accredited, exclusively online MBA program.

Eschewing the traditional semester system, JIU offers students rolling enrollment in courses that last for 16 or eight (accelerated) weeks and which are based on one hour of contact time per week. Tuition at JIU is approximately $500 to $700 per course. With no traditional campus, JIU offers its students the services of an online librarian with access to Internet databases and reference collections. Most JIU students are enrolled in non-degree courses or certificate programs.

North Central's decision in 1999 to accredit JIU generated considerable controversy. From the perspective of Robert C. Albrecht, chief academic officer at Western

Governors University, JIU's accreditation was important because it "gives more credibility to all virtual institutions." Critics of NCA's decision, on the other hand, were outraged. The most widely circulated critique of the NCA action came from the American Association of University Professors (AAUP). James Perley, chair of AAUP's committee on accrediting, in a letter to the executive director of NCA, cited the lack of full-time faculty members at JIU, who would be expected to shape the curriculum, uphold the quality of teaching and research, and mentor and advise JIU students. Perley also raised objections to JIU's prepackaged courses, the institution's one online reference librarian and JIU's overreliance on parttime faculty. As Perley explained, "By all public accounts, [JIU] presents a very weak case for accreditation. Indeed it embodies most of our major worries about the denigration of quality that could follow this apparently inexorable march toward online education."

At a June 1995 meeting of the Western Governors Association, policymakers discussed the issue of population growth in the West and the potential for rapidly expanding enrollment at regional colleges and universities. In response, the governors created the Western Governors University, one of the most highly publicized virtual universities created in the past few years. Organized as a joint project of 19 western states and Guam, WGU is a privately owned university that offers courses from a range of outside academic institutions and corporations.

In 1997, WGU officials signed collaborative agreements with the British Open University, the Open Learning Agency (British Columbia), Tokai University (Japan) and the Universidad Virtual del Instituto Tecnologico y de Estudio

Superiores de Monterrey (Mexico). These institutions would provide courses for students in pursuit of WGU's competency-based degrees and certificates. In 1998, WGU began offering three degree and certificate programs.

WGU's competency-based education has generated controversy. Under this system, students can gain credits toward their degree or certificate by demonstrating mastery, in lieu of actual coursework, in a particular field. Students can demonstrate their knowledge of a particular field via standardized test, portfolio, research paper or any number of other assessments. Theoretically, students could earn an entire degree without actually sitting through even one course.

WGU currently offers competency-based associate of applied science degrees in aspects of instructional technology, associate's and bachelor's degrees in business, and an M.A. in learning and technology. In November 2000, Western Governors University was granted candidate status for accreditation by the Inter-Regional Accrediting Committee (IRAC), which is composed of representatives from four regional accrediting agencies.

WGU claims to have a "distributed" faculty, meaning that the institution does not hire its own teaching faculty and relies on its affiliates. The university Web site reports that "traditional faculty roles" at WGU are "unbundled." According to the WGU Web site, "Program council members oversee the curriculum, assessment council members assure the tests and measures are accurate and effective, and mentors work with students to design the path to achieve their goals."

The larger problem at WGU has been low enrollment (the college enrolled only 208 students in 1999-2000), which one analyst attributed to student concerns over the perceived quality of WGU's competency-based degrees and certificates. In September 2000, the state of Utah released an audit that criticized WGU for its low enrollment numbers, for withholding information from auditors, and for overcharging students for degree programs in comparison with other regional colleges and universities.

Capella University, based in Minneapolis, is a private, virtual university geared toward adult professionals. Founded in 1993 by CEO Steve Shank, Capella has instituted faculty and student policies that are more in line with existing brickand- mortar institutions. Although the large majority of Capella's 170 faculty members work part time, individual faculty, for example, teach their own courses, and the university maintains a maximum of 12 students per course. Capella students, moreover, are required "to interact with one another and with their instructors at least once a week online," a policy designed to alleviate concerns over the lack of meaningful interaction with faculty at other virtual universities.

With a current enrollment of 3,000 students, Capella is expected to become profitable by 2002. Capella offers undergraduate degree programs in information technology as well as graduate and Ph.D. programs in business, education, human services and psychology. In April 2000, Capella University was accredited by the North Central Association. Other examples of virtual universities include Kennedy-Western University, which maintains an office in Cheyenne Wyo. and Andrew Jackson University, based in Birmingham Ala. Kennedy-Western markets distance education courses to "mid-career" professionals seeking a degree in business, education or engineering. It was recently highlighted in The

Chronicle of Higher Education as one of many online institutions that lacked regional accreditation. Licensed only by the Wyoming State Department of Education, Kennedy-Western is barred from enrolling California students and has been contacted by the Oregon attorney general's office for misleading advertising in that state. Robin Dodson, chief academic officer for the Idaho State Board of Education, which also rejected an application by Kennedy-Western, says that many of Kennedy-Western's students are located overseas. The college purports to have offices in Jakarta, Indonesia, as well as Moscow and Singapore.

Andrew Jackson University has a decidedly lowtech approach toward distance education. Although the institution maintains an up-to-date Web site, its curriculum is based on textbook study. AJU markets itself as the online university for religious home-schooled students. Its teacher-practitioner faculty produces the institution's study guides and course examinations in each degree program. It is unclear whether they have direct contact with students. AJU is accredited by the Accrediting Commission of the Distance Education and Training Council (DETC), which is recognized by the U.S. Department of Education as a national accrediting agency. Formerly known as the National Home Study Council, the DETC accredits more than 70 institutions that offer home study, even though credits from DETC-accredited institutions are not widely accepted at regionally accredited colleges and universities.

Corporate University or Training Institutions

Corporate managers have had a long history of involvement in American higher education. Beginning in the late 19th century, many prominent corporations organized in-house training institutes for their workers. Westinghouse created its in-house school in 1888, General Electric in 1901. Generally, the more technologically sophisticated the industry, the greater the chance that corporations would create their own training programs.In 1913, representatives from 34 different firms founded the National Association of Corporation Schools, laying the foundation for what Dan Schiller calls a "shadow system" of corporate postsecondary education in the United States.

By 1980, there were hundreds of corporate universities in existence. Today, according to Jeanne Meister, president of the Corporate University Xchange, there are more then 2,000 corporate universities worldwide. These include corporate training schools that have existed for many years, such as the ITT Technical Institute, Sylvan Learning Systems or DeVry, as well as a legion of recent startups and new exclusively distance education providers such as Smartforce, Skillsoft and Digitalthink, and infrastructure providers Saba and Docent.

Another prominent example of a new and expanding corporate content provider is Click2-learn, founded by Microsoft co-founder Paul Alan. Click2learn maintains a very large catalog of online courses for business and professional training, and it has an extensive corporate, university and government national accrediting agency. Formerly known as the National Home Study Council, the DETC accredits more than 70 institutions that offer home study, even though credits from DETC-accredited institutions are not widely accepted at regionally accredited colleges and universities.

Corporate University or Training Institutions

Corporate managers have had a long history of involvement in American higher education. Beginning in the late 19th century, many prominent corporations organized in-house training institutes for their workers. Westinghouse created its in-house school in 1888, General Electric in 1901. Generally, the more technologically sophisticated the industry, the greater the chance that corporations would create their own training programs.

In 1913, representatives from 34 different firms founded the National Association of Corporation Schools, laying the foundation for what Dan Schiller calls a "shadow system" of corporate postsecondary education in the United States.

By 1980, there were hundreds of corporate universities in existence. Today, according to Jeanne Meister, president of the Corporate University Xchange, there are more then 2,000 corporate universities worldwide. These include corporate training schools that have existed for many years, such as the ITT Technical Institute, Sylvan Learning Systems or DeVry, as well as a legion of recent startups and new exclusively distance education providers such as Smartforce, Skillsoft and Digitalthink, and infrastructure providers Saba and Docent.

Another prominent example of a new and expanding corporate content provider is Click2-learn, founded by Microsoft co-founder Paul Alan. Click2learn maintains a very large catalog of online courses for business and professional training, and it has an extensive corporate, university and government agency client list. Today, the average corporate university is four years old, has an annual budget of $15 million, employs 79 full-time employees and delivers 23 percent of the corporation's annual training via DE. Corporations have increasingly utilized DE for training needs because it makes travel and accommodations unnecessary. According to *Training* magazine, hotel and travel costs make up two-thirds of the total cost of corporate training annually.

With the advent of DE and the centralization of corporate training and executive development departments within separate institutions, some corporate universities have reached the point of being nearly indistinguishable from other, for-profit online business schools. Motorola University, one of the largest corporate schools, perhaps best illustrates this blurring of once-clear boundaries.With a faculty of 400 full-time instructors and 800 parttime contract teachers, and a "student body" of 100,000 workers per year, the accredited Motorola U. rivals large state universities in size, reach and budget.

The rise of the corporate university phenomenon has impacted traditional higher education in immeasurable ways. The explosion of corporate universities has provided opportunities for faculty members as instructors and content providers. Many corporate universities have formed partnerships with existing higher education institutions as method of gaining access to the educational "seal of approval" offered by regional or national accrediting agencies. Although some corporate universities have begun directly competing with traditional colleges and universities and offering courses to the general public, only a few have undertaken the arduous task of applying for accreditation.

The pace of distance education is accelerating, and it is likely to occupy a growing part of the landscape in higher education. But if the report signals expansion, it also demonstrates that *the way* distance education is being organized and conducted may pose serious questions. Much of the distance education described in these pages. whether nonprofit or for-profit, is built on ideas drawn from the corporate sector about consumer focus, product standardization, tight personnel control and costeffectiveness (that is, to maximize course taking while minimizing the "inputs" of faculty and development time).

These ideas, oriented to the corporate world. do not reflect the traditional model of higher education decision-making which emphasizes faculty independence in teaching and research, academic control of the curriculum, academic freedom in the classroom and collegial decision-making. We are not suggesting that corporate ideas are always wrong or that the way things have always been done is the way they should be done forever.

However, we strongly believe that broad academic content, high standards, personal interaction and professional control are the key elements of educational quality. Academic decision-making processes have done a good job of producing these elements of quality—the best in the world—and we are concerned that some of the trends and practices described in the preceding sections may inhibit rather than promote the basics of good education.

AFT quality principles and distance education

The importance of maintaining educational quality has been AFT's primary message since distance education emerged as a major issue in the mid-1990s. In 1996, the AFT published its first report on the subject, Teaming Up with Technology, which alerted unions to the necessity of involving themselves in all aspects of DE decision-making. The report urged unions to focus their involvement around four key questions: Does the technology make sense educationally? Does it make sense financially? Do students and faculty all have access to new technologies and know how to use them? Are faculty and staff rights protected? A number of reports analyzing distance education trends followed. In 2000, AFT deepened its involvement with the publication of Distance Education: Guidelines for *Good Practice* which offers a set of 14 benchmarks for achieving quality in the distance environment. A summary of the *Guidelines* appears on page 19.

AFT believes that excellent distance education can take place under any organizational structure—public and private institutions, even the newer profit-making models—if these guidelines are scrupulously observed. In fact, faculty members nationwide today are conducting distance courses of the highest quality. It was the experience and advice of DE faculty that shaped AFT's standards focused on strong academic content, interaction and professional control. The problem, however, is that a number of serious questions and concerns arise when we measure our quality principles against many practices outlined in the previous pages. Here are some of those issues.

DE trends and practices

1. *The marketplace and the curriculum*: Most of the models outlined in this report emphasize meeting immediate market demands for coursework as well as treating students primarily as "customers." It is entirely appropriate to consider student and industry preferences in designing curricula, particularly in the corporate training arena.

However, we believe that the pre-eminent perspective should be that of academic professionals rather than the marketplace. One concern is that the pure "student as consumer" model rests on the questionable assumption that student-consumers know what they want when they begin an educational program and can confidently decide what courses will lead to the desired educational "product." Another concern is that broad-based liberal arts coursework, as well as high academic standards, could take a back seat if market models become dominant.

2. *Technological capabilities and the curriculum:* In one of the stories cited earlier, a distance education advocate explained that professors will have to curb their lectures in order to fit their ideas into a 256-character dialogue box. This raises serious questions. Technological capabilities and limitations should not be the primary factor driving the curriculum and research required of distance education students, rather than the rich interplay among research, curriculum and good pedagogy.

3. *Faculty decision-making*: To ensure that academic decisions are made for academic reasons, a key characteristic of quality in distance education is ensuring that faculty are in control of shaping and approving courses and integrating them into a coherent curriculum. This is the number one item in AFT's Guidelines for Good Practice. Another basic precept is academic freedom; an individual faculty member should have the authority to determine how the class will be taught.

We are concerned, however, that many of the programs described above appear to keep authority to develop course content confined to a very narrow circle. Some models directly challenge the idea of academic freedom in the classroom. For example, at the University of Phoenix, we saw that course "facilitators" not only are forbidden to lecture, but also must follow detailed teaching modules.

4. *Disaggregation:* Many of the institutions reviewed here are moving to a model of curriculum development and teaching that "unbundles" the many roles of the faculty member. A process that has traditionally been maintained from start to finish by the individual faculty member is being parted into specializations—curriculum developers, content deliverers, assessment specialists, etc. This can be seen most starkly in movements such as "The National Learning Infrastructure Initiative" (NLII) created in 1994 by Educom (now Educause), a coalition of technology corporations, public and private colleges and universities and higher education organizations.

Specifically, the NLII would increase student access through the construction of a broadband network modeled on the Internet. The program would be characterized by self-paced study instead of academic calendars, fixed class meetings or a traditional curriculum. Students would pursue their studies via new instructional software that breaks down complex subjects into individual components or modules.

In 1996, Educom released a report on "The Virtual University," which envisions the resulting new role for faculty and the benefits for the institution. [In the virtual university], the many roles previously combined in a single faculty member are now disaggregated. Faculty may specialize as developers of courses and courseware wherein they move from being content experts to being a combination of content expert, learning-process design expert, and process-implementation manager; as presenters of that material; as expert assessors of learning and competencies; as advisors; or as specialists in other evolving roles.In this view, one of the main advantages of the NLII is that it would "reduce faculty intervention, thereby containing costs." As Massy and Zemsky explain:

> Workstations don't get tenure, and delegations are less likely to wait on the provost when particular equipment items are "laid off." The "retraining" of IT equipment (for example, reprogramming), while not inexpensive, is easier and more predictable than training a tenured professor.

Many providers in all four categories have embraced this vision to differing extents, but the AFT believes this is not the best route to quality. Quoting directly from the AFT *Guidelines:* A number of studies have demonstrated the importance to student learning of establishing a feedback loop between classroom teaching, curriculum development and scholarly research. That loop becomes inoperative when teaching faculty operate from workbooks based on a prefabricated curriculum that the faculty member has little role in developing, a curriculum that was not shaped directly by the practitioner's experience in teaching these classes or conducting research on these subjects. Students deserve teachers who know all the nuances of what they are teaching and who can exercise professional judgment and academic freedom in doing so.

5. *Course standardization:* Many of the providers outlined above are attracted to the idea of creating consistent and

transferable courses by utilizing course management software and course development specialists. The idea is that an institution or set of institutions can make all of their courses have the same look and feel, and that courses can and should be designed for longevity and transferability. If course management software such as Web CT or Blackboard simply provide faculty with greater technical support and facilitate the faculty member's pedagogy, then they will be powerful teaching aids. But standardization in programming and teaching is the wrong way to go; academic good practice requires a faculty with differing points of view and presentation styles, freewheeling discussion and academic freedom.

6. *Class Size:* AFT's distance education practitioners report that good DE generally requires more teacher preparation time than a traditional class as well as more time devoted to interacting with students (through e-mail, chat rooms, etc.) Therefore, it is important to maintain a workable class size. The concern, however, is that commercially minded DE will expand class sizes too greatly in order to maximize enrollments. The move on the part of some providers to concentrate on offering high-enrollment introductory courses (such as introductory psychology) is of particular concern because DE practitioners tell us the students best suited to succeed in a distance education environment are not the newcomers but those who are more mature, better prepared and able to work independently.

Increasing class size is an integral part of the Pew grants at Rio Salado College cited earlier. Introductory algebra, which had the third highest enrollment of the top 25 courses in the district, was selected for redesign. Course content was delivered via interactive software. The restructuring increased the student/faculty ratio from 35 to 100 students per instructor, although each faculty member was assigned teaching assistants to help with technology questions, and students had access to a help desk. AFT's *Guidelines* recommend that class size be established through normal faculty channels, with a view to maintaining a high level of interactivity. "Given the time commitment involved in teaching through distance education," say the *Guidelines*, "smaller class size should be considered, particularly at the inception of a new course."

7. *"Outcomes" and Class Time*: The Western Governors University emphasis on "proficiencies" is the most extreme version of this shift. A greater emphasis on outcomes may be warranted, but a critical question remains: Will an exclusive focus on measurable outputs shortchange the importance of *process* and interactivity in higher education?

Distance education advocates often deride what they call "seat time"—the practice of requiring students to be together and work together for periods of time before passing their courses. Under their theory, if a student can demonstrate "competencies," it should not matter how much time is spent achieving these competencies. The AFT, however, believes that deep knowledge of a subject is not simply a matter of passing a competency test. It does in fact require time—time in the same room or in cyberspace—with teachers and other students chewing over ideas, hearing contrary points of view and defending conclusions. There is reason for concern if time on task comes to be viewed as a luxury rather than a necessity in DE on the corporate model.

8. *Same-time, same-place interaction:* There is no denying that rich interaction can take place in distance education classes, but we believe it is equally untenable to argue that same-time, sameplace interaction has no legitimate role in an undergraduate education. We believe distance education should utilize every available opportunity to bring students and faculty together at some time during an academic program. Our concern is that providing such opportunities does not appear to be a consideration for most of the providers we have studied. It is particularly troubling to have no sametime, same-place interchange through an entire undergraduate program. AFT faculty who teach by distance education have reported to the union that they believe same-time, same-place interaction should be part of any undergraduate program. In fact, more than 70 percent say that no more than half of a full undergraduate program should be delivered via distance education.

It is proper, even necessary, for higher education faculty to make distance education work, but that may often mean contradicting current DE practice to affirm academic values. Faculty must mobilize behind the principle that democratic governance rather than top-down management produces better, more credible education. Faculty must ensure that college degrees are awarded in the context of a coordinated curriculum with broad-based content. Faculty must see to it that students have the equipment, training and support to succeed in the distance education environment and that they have appropriate academic counseling. Faculty must make the case that time *does* matter—that education is not simply a matter of passing a competency test but, whether in the same room or far apart, being with other teachers and students chewing over ideas, hearing contrary points of view and defending conclusions. Faculty must assert and find ways to implement the notion that same-time, same-place interchange is an important part of a college education. Faculty must always affirm the importance of free exchange of ideas.

In short, faculty must insist on sound practice based on a broad vision of education—one that recognizes education is about more than facts, more than competencies, more than career ambitions—the things that can be easily "sold." Education is about broadening one's intellectual horizons, learning to rely on facts and reason rather than on prejudices when confronting life issues. It is about learning to listen to others and defend ideas by the force of argument. It is about learning respect and acquiring openmindedness, and as such, education is the foundation of a working democracy.

Distance education can make an important contribution toward achieving these goals if it is organized around practices such as those in AFT's Distance Education: Guidelines for Good Practice. However, no one should imagine that implementing these guidelines will be easy in a world where the promise of big dollars and big enrollments constantly beckons. AFT and its members, other organizations representing the faculty and, of course, individual faculty members themselves, will have to be prepared to take up the charge for quality.

6

Costs of Net-oriented Education

Until the late 1950s there was relatively little interest in the costs of education, and virtually none in the costs of educational technology. This failure reflected the fact that innovation in teaching methods was a largely marginal activity: as one early analyst put it, 'education's technology, by and large, has made surprisingly little progress beyond the handicraft stage'.

However, the rising demand for and escalating costs of education led to attempts within the newly developing sub-discipline of the economics of education to quantify both the efficiency of public expenditure on education, and the economic benefits of providing it. Educational technology came to be seen as a way of improving the efficiency of education through productivity increases. As a result analysts began to research into the costing of educational technology and the actual costs of distance education systems.

Much of the early work undertaken under the auspices of the World Bank, UNESCO and USAID focused on the costs and cost structures of educational broadcasting projects. Within the UK other experts focused on the costs of using educational technology either for distance teaching or as a substitute for classroom teaching on campus. Some of this work was developed further in Australia within the context of universities mixing traditional and distance education approaches.

The development of networked learning has once again raised similar questions as policy makers and analysts ask both whether networked learning is cheaper or more expensive than other approaches to education, and what needs to be taken into account in costing such systems.

The key to much of the early work lies in the attempt to identify clearly the nature of the costs involved, and what drives them, so that not only can all the relevant costs be taken into account, but also their behavior within planned or actual systems can be modelled.

So far as the nature of the costs are concerned, most studies adopt the conventional distinction between capital costs (buildings, equipment and furniture) which are annualized over their expected life, and revenue costs. The latter are normally categorized as staffing costs (including on-costs) and non-staffing costs (covering revenue expenditures on premises, stocks, supplies, consumables, and expenses).

Generally capital costs have been regarded as non-recurrent costs – though the short life of some capital items, particularly in the IT area, means that institutions are increasingly treating such budgets as a recurrent item that is treated in much the same way as revenue budgets are. On the other hand, revenue expenditure on the development of course materials (which involves considerable expenditure on labor) in fact behaves very much like capital expenditure, incurred when the course is designed but expected to retain some value over the expected life of the course. While annualisation of traditional capital costs is commonplace, the annualisation of course development costs is less so.

The failure to annualise course development costs is problematic given that the length of life over which courses last is a major factor in the overall efficiency of technology-based education. At the macro-level the costs of any system are driven by a combination of the following factors, all of which are susceptible to management control:

— Course populations

— The number of courses offered

— The lengths of course lifetimes

— The media and technologies chosen

— The extent to which cost-inducing actions, for example, the use of copyrighted materials, are avoided

— The extent to which costs are placed on students, either as tuition, or by moving the system boundaries so that activities the institution might once have paid for are now paid for by students (e.g. access to tutorial and library services)

— The extent to which the institution employs people on contracts *for* service (i.e. salaried posts) to develop courses and teach students, rather than on contracts *of* service (i.e. hired as casual labor, to be paid by the manuscript/script/tutorial hour/test marked, etc.)

— The extent to which the institution adopts working practices that reduce the costs of labor by, for example, designing courses to be wrapped-around existing textbooks rather than developing new materials, and using author-editor models of course design, rather than big course team models

— The use of technology to increase the student load per academic or administrator

— Increases in the teaching load of academic staff at the expense of other functions – for example, research and public service, and ...

— 'Labor for labor' substitution – the replacement of expensive academic labor by student and adjunct labor, in order to reduce staff costs.

An important element in costing is to understand the system being costed so that cost elements are not missed. Far too many analysts restrict their analysis to their own budget. Of course, understanding one's own budget and controlling it is important. The answers one obtains to questions such as 'How much will this cost me?' and 'Will doing it this way cost more or less than doing it that way?' will help one decide whether, from a purely parochial interest, one should or should not proceed with a given course of action.

However, the wider one's span of interest, the more one will want to look at the macro-picture. Individual teachers may be content to find out whether teaching online, for example, takes them more or less time than teaching face-to-face, but departmental heads will want to know whether they can teach more courses and/or more students per course, and what the effect will be on their expenditure and their income. Institutional heads will be concerned with all the above questions, but will also want to know what the impact is on administrative costs, while institutional heads and national educational planners may want to know whether teaching online is cheaper or more expensive than teaching face-to-face or by some other distance teaching methodology.

Students will want to know whether taking a course online adds to their costs, or saves them money and/or time – and actually academics, course leaders, and institutional leaders should care deeply about student costs, since student decisions on whether or not to study with a particular institution will be driven in part by cost considerations. These considerations will go beyond the cost of tuition to cover the costs of engaging with the course. This argues for a whole systems approach to the costing of projects that moves beyond the immediate concerns of individual course and departmental budgets to take account of the cost implications of the system as a whole on overhead functions and the customer.

The use of learning materials has already resulted in a sharp temporal differentiation between the design and delivery phases of the activity of teaching, with the design and production of complex multi-media courses beginning many months before they are taught, thus separating these activities in time (and often across budget years).

Once created, the materials can be packaged in various ways and used, often for a number of years, on a range of different courses. They can also be used by very large numbers of students. All this makes it less likely that a single member of faculty will control the whole teaching-learning process from materials design through to delivery. On large population courses the chances are that not only will most of the actual interaction and assessment of students have to be farmed out to auxiliary teachers, but much of the administration of the teaching-learningassessment process will also be handed to professionals whose task it will be to seek economies of scale and process.

Division of labor between those who design the materials, those who teach the courses, and those who administer and support student progress, follows. Indeed, the capital nature of the costs expended on course development, the division of labor that occurs in many systems, and the fact that materials once developed may be repackaged for use on a number of courses, argue for a clear distinction to be made between materials development and course delivery. To date issues around the division of labor have been seen most clearly in distance education – most notably in large-scale 'first generation' correspondence systems, and in 'second generation' educational broadcasting and 'third generation' multi-media systems.

This 'Fordist' tendency has been greatly criticized by those who see it as a reflection of the increasing degradation of academic work. It has been suggested that just as cottage-industry correspondence systems can be run by faculty who retain control over the whole teaching-learning process, so the development of online education allows faculty to teach at a distance without losing control of their course – and indeed this is true in some cases.

However, a division of labor is likely to occur because in the long run any system that limits control of design and delivery to a single person limits both the range and sophistication of the materials that can be developed, and the number of students that can be supported, and is thus inherently cost-inefficient given the much greater economies of scale and process achievable in systems designed around the division of labor.

In addition, a range of more immediately personal issues arises for faculty involved in the development of materials. For example, will such an academic have to continue to teach traditional students in class at the same time as he or she develops the internet course? Will he/she be given time off to compensate them for the time spent developing the course, and if so who will help teach the traditional course? Will he/she be given no immediate help in the development of the course, but then be allowed – as happens in the French system – to substitute resource-based learning for personal teaching in the delivery phase, thus freeing up time that can then be spent on other more personal objectives (such as research and public service)?

To these issues must be added issues around the actual teaching of online courses, including such issues as the evolution of new academic roles such as e-moderating, and the extent to which teaching online requires more or less time of academics.

So far we have focused on the use of the network for academic purposes – in essence as the location through which ethereal (i.e. non-physical) course materials can be accessed, and as the site through which electronic dialogue and discourse takes place. But a fully developed e-education system would use the network and website as the location for the administration of the learners' progress through the institution – that is, as the site through which students would electronically enrol, pay for their courses, change their records, and seek general counselling and advise. The development and maintenance of a web site to support academic and administrative functions must therefore be seen as an integral part of the provision of an e-education system, and hence of part of the costs of the system.

Those working within the teaching institution will of course be able to access the web site easily through the institution's own network – but remote tutors and students also need access to the web site. This generally means providing their own computing equipment and connections to the web –though occasionally an institution may help by setting up tele-learning centers where students (and tutors) can make use of institutional equipment to access the site. Either way, the costs of access/reception are an integral part of the system as a whole, and need to be taken into account, if not for budgeting purposes, then at least for purposes of cost analysis.

On top of these elements are the costs of managing an e-education system. In virtual education institutions these overhead costs will be obvious, but in dual mode systems there is the possibility that these costs can be set aside, at least for a while, in order to give the e-education system a 'free' ride. Such free rides will not survive expansion, nor can they be ignored in cases where comparative costings between online and other systems are being attempted.

Thus the institutional costs of a fully developed e-education systems would include:

1. Developing e-materials
2. Teaching (and assessing) students online
3. Accessing the web site

4. Administering students online
5. Providing the infrastructure and support within which e-education can operate
6. Planning and managing e-education at the macro-level.

However, one is likely to find that the range of costs is very great. This arises in part because there are very different ideas as to what online learning actually is – varying from those who see it in terms of access to materials and to assessment schemes that favor multiple choice formats, to those who stress the communicative and constructivist nature of the dialogue that can occur between teacher and students, and among students. These different expectations of online learning are reflected in the costs of systems, making it hard to come to any concrete conclusions about their costs.

Costing of Online Learning

In the light of the development of networked learning, a new generation of academics, interested in the impact of online learning on the costs of education, has begun to evolve a methodology by which to approach the task of costing such systems. None of these studies provides a wholly comprehensive approach to the costs of networked learning. Such an approach would require an analysis that looked at the costs of a system:

(a) by *expenditure category* (using the traditional distinctions between human resource or staff costs, premises and accommodation costs, equipment and furniture costs, and the costs of stocks, supplies, consumables and expenses), and

(b) by *contributor* (e.g. the institution's own budget, partner institutions' inputs, direct government inputs, aid agency inputs, staff inputs, and student inputs), while

(c) distinguishing between *capital* and *revenue costs*, with the former, including the investment in course materials, annualized over their expected life, and

(d) where this seems sensible to the analyst, using an appropriate systems framework for the analysis of costs.

If this provides a framework for the analysis of the costs of online learning, the next issue must be, exactly what kinds of costs are being identified, and how should they be treated? The first thing to say is that *all* the relevant costs should be identified. Secondly, costs should not be netted off from income since this hides the full costs involved. In fact, examination of the work done to date shows that the different analysts:

— Lack agreement on the costs that should be taken into account. This is particularly the case with regards to overhead costs (i.e. the costs analysed here within the regulatory and logistics subsystems) that are, in general, ignored.

— Employ very different labels or terms to describe what they are costing. This reflects jurisdictional and linguistic differences in terminology, local institutional practice, and personal preferences.

— Aggregate or disaggragate costs in different ways.

— Employ a variety of frameworks to give coherence to their work.

Costs of Online Learning

The major costs of e-education can be usefully considered under the three heads identified above – viz. the costs of developing web-based materials, the costs of e-education delivery, and the overhead costs of embarking on e-education.

Costs of Developing e-materials

Most of the technologies involved in Web-based courses have been around for a long time. They include the preparation of text, audio, video, computer-based tutoring, intelligent tutoring, exploratory learning, simulations, etc. What is distinctive is that these materials are now being put on a web site that can then be accessed by students.

For many years distance educators have known that not only do media and technologies have their own cost structures, but also that some media are more expensive than others. Bates's analysis of the costs of various media concluded that print, audio-cassettes, and pre-recorded Instructional Television are the only media that are relatively low cost for courses with populations of from under 250 students a year to over 1000 student a year.

In addition, radio is also likely to be low cost on courses with populations of 1000 or more students. Hülsmann, on the basis of his study of the costs of 11 courses offered by 9 different European distance teaching organisations, argues that at £350 per student learning hour print is the cheapest medium to develop. Putting text up on the internet costs at least twice that, and possibly more. After that costs escalate through audio (£1,700), CD-ROM (£13,000), video (£35,000) and TV (£121,000).

These figures are based on averages across eleven courses in nine institutions, and hence need to be treated with care, given the wide variations in costs encountered in practice. However, the broad differences in media costs are carried through into the development of internet-based courses. Arizona Learning Systems found a wide variation in the costs of developing a course, of from US$6000 to $1,000,000 for a three unit internet course, depending on the approach used. Much of this is the cost of academic and technical labor. The cheapest approach involved the presentation of simple course outlines and assignments; the most expensive, at $1,000,000, involved virtual reality.

The high costs of developing internet courses are confirmed by Saba, who suggests that commercial software companies developing courses for online instruction or publishers are spending at least $500,000 to fully develop a multimedia course.

There is some evidence that the lower levels of cost are more likely to be found on synchronous online courses, with asynchronous courses costing more. Certainly Whalen and Wright found significant differences between synchronous and asynchronous course development costs. The former required much less development time because they involved fewer media.

A high proportion of the costs of developing materials is labor costs. All the research shows that it takes more academic time to develop media that will occupy a student for one hour, than it takes to develop a one hour lecture – although how much more time is difficult to quantify. Sparkes reckoned that it took from 2 to 10 hours to prepare a lecture, from 1 to 10 hours to prepare a small group session, and from 3 to 10 hours to prepare a video-tape lecture; however, it took at least 50 to 100 academic hours to prepare a teaching text, 100 hours to prepare a television broadcast, 200 hours to develop computer-aided leaming, and 300 hours to develop interactive materials – to which in all cases one needed to add the time of technical support staff.

Boettcher suggests that it takes an average of about 18 hours faculty time to create an hour of instruction online. Academic development costs can be reduced or at least kept in check by adopting cheaper approaches to course development – for example, author-editor models based on an editor working with consultant authors, instead of hiring permanent staff.

One of the problems with many of the studies now available is that they report the broad results, not the detail. It is therefore difficult to know what has been included and what excluded, and so whether the costings undertaken are comprehensive. Experience suggests, however, that all figures need to be treated with care. What does seem clear is that the costs of developing a course are being pushed up –and significantly so whenever media are used in a sophisticated way. If so, and if cost efficiency is an important consideration, then savings may need to be looked for in delivery.

Costs of e-delivery

Although the development costs of even relatively simple online materials may be higher than paperbased print, it seems fairly clear that there are considerable institutional savings on delivery costs. The Library of Virginia has digitized the state's colonial records. This has drastically reduced the costs of fulfilling requests from readers. The costs to the library of providing a single copy of a four page report in digital format is just 90 US cents, compared with $19 to supply a surface-mail customer, and $12 to supply an on-site user.

Applied to course materials, online delivery to order could cut inventory, packing, and postage costs enormously. Online library services like those offered or under development by XanEdu and Questia are likely to be invaluable – provided the subscription rates that users are to be charged are not unreasonably high. However, students used to their course materials dropping through their letterboxes are likely to see their study costs rise as they access and perhaps pay for materials online, and print them off themselves.

What about the costs of computer-mediated communications and assessment? Here we get into the costs of labor and the problems of student load. Bates has suggested that in comparison with face-toface teaching, CMC will lower the costs of tuition because a good deal of the students' time is spent studying the material, and so the teacher needs to spend less time per student overall in class. Other analysts argue that students will also spend a great deal more time learning from their peers, and that this too will reduce the demands they make of their tutors.

Certainly DiBiase, teaching for Penn State University's World Campus, found that he and his Teaching Assistant were spending less time supporting students on an online course (1.6 hours per student against 2.6 hours on a regular course).

However, the general consensus seems to be that online tutoring adds to traditional faculty workload given the enormous volume of messaging arising from increased interaction with students, with each message requiring more time to compose than is the case in verbal interactions. For faculty, teaching online opens up the possibility that they are always in session – which translates into 'taking more time'.

Moonen thinks that the increased load would be of the order of 5 to 10 hours a week for a class of 60 to 120 students. Jewett thinks tutors could well spend twice as much time tutoring online as they do face-to-face. This raises the question of how many students an online instructor can handle. In classroom courses in the USA it looks as if people think they can handle from 25 to 30 students, working perhaps 10 to 12 hours a week.

Boettcher suggests that experience indicates that a member of faculty can handle more students on a web course – in the range 25 to 65, but that this will require more time – so that although there are courses with 50 – 60 students on them, there are many courses where student numbers are deliberately kept down, somewhere in the range of from 12 to 20 students.

One way of coping with an academic's increased workload is to hire more staff but this, of course, costs more. However, the impact on labor costs can be reduced through 'labor-for-labor' substitution – that is, the substitution of cheap labor for expensive faculty labor. This cheap labor might be students, teaching assistants, or clerks covering help desks. These options are much discussed in the US literature. However, hiring cheaper labor is not possible in small classes run by just one academic; it only works in large classes. Also, labor-for-labor substitution has its critics. Traditionally PhD students have helped teach courses but student labor is not the cheapest labor on offer. Adjunct staff hired by the class is even less expensive – so much so that there is concern that their employment could damage graduate programmes by reducing the employment opportunities for PhD students.

What about CMC's impact on the costs of distance education delivery? Firstly, there is evidence that distance tutors spend more time moderating and tutoring e-courses. Tolley, drawing on her experience as a UK Open University tutor, found that she spent more than twice as many hours tutoring the online version of *What is Europe?* as she did the 'traditional' version – 120 hours against 48. She was not paid for the additional work, which also had a dramatic effect on her 'phone bill. Annand, from his perspective at Athabasca University, suggests that it is these costs that may in the end constrain the extent to which large-scale distance teaching universities can adopt online technologies. Some institutions are trying to find ways of containing demands on tutor time by controlling student expectations and limiting the time for engagement on a particular topic; others, like the e-University, might subcontract tutoring to commercial ventures like Tutor.com, which will charge students for the service.

Secondly, there are the costs of reception. Cost analysis tends to be bounded by the institutional budget. The costs students incur in acquiring and operating equipment is not generally taken into account – yet from the would-be student's point of view, these costs can have a major impact on affordability, and hence on access. In the USA the distribution of computers is highly graduated by income, race/ethnicity, and educational attainment. In the Third World, the situation is much worse. If owning the equipment is a necessary condition for participation, then expect to see more disadvantaged people being excluded on cost grounds.

Local centers may, of course, mitigate student costs by providing access to machines, but they cost a fair amount in rent, equipment, furniture and staffing to set up – and generally accommodate very few students at any one time. This is not a solution to mass access – which is why the African Virtual University is such a limited project. Internet cafés cost money to use and are not necessarily ideal environments for study. In any case, in a country like Uganda, anything that uses a telephone line is extremely expensive.

The assumption behind many of the cases put forward to support the development of e-teaching is that the technology will substitute for the labor costs of teaching. Students will, it is assumed, spend a lot more of their time studying independently from the materials, and much less time in formal classes.

One potential advantage is that this will make more faculty time available for students to discuss with their teachers what they have learnt independently – but if so, any savings in faculty time disappear and are likely to be at most modest . If there are no savings on faculty time, then the argument begins to focus on balancing the additional technology costs against sometimes more tenuous accommodation savings – which is not to say that some projects such as the Florida Gulf Coast University do not hope to make substantial savings on building costs. In any case, as Massy and Zemsky comment, actually achieving capital for labor substitutions may prove difficult for many colleges.

One other factor is the extent to which faculty are properly reimbursed for the costs they incur when teaching online. Schifter reports the very wide range of practice that occurs. Her analysis suggests that many distance teachers do not have their costs reimbursed. Generally speaking, there are powerful incentives to bring the costs of teaching down. In a situation where the technology, far from reducing contact hours, may be actually increasing faculty hours spent in contact with students, there are powerful pressures to reduce faculty labor costs by substituting cheaper for more expensive labor. This does not always replace experienced by inexperienced staff; some systems go out of their way to hire recently retired faculty who are looking to supplement their incomes. Nevertheless, the fact remains that the pressure is on to reduce costs.

Mass education distance teaching universities such as Britain's Open University, with some courses having over 10,000 students enrolled at the same time, have had to employ models based on a division of labor between those who develop the course materials, those who teach/tutor, and those who mark examination scripts. Not surprisingly the Open University employs its tutors and script markers on contracts of service. Institutions that restrict the number of students taking distance courses do not have the same problem. Certainly with the exception of a few institutions such as the non-traditional University of Phoenix, practice in America has generally not led to any systematic restructuring of academic labor force. Nevertheless, a general increase in the use of adjunct and part-time faculty has been noted, while the pressures to massify *and* reduce costs must give managers an incentive to hire casual labor.

Another factor at play here is the extent to which costs that used to be met by the teaching institution – or at least were wrapped up in the tuition fees charged – are now being pushed on to students quite overtly.

Costs of E-administration

We know very little about the costs of e-administration, but on the whole this may be the area where savings are most likely to occur. Service costs in a range of industries are being brought down as institutions invert traditional processes, such as student services, to focus more on Web-based, selfservice models.

A paper-based order costs about $65 to fulfil – but it only costs around $5 to fulfil an online order. A paper-based invoice may cost US$0.90 to produce and distribute; online services can reduce this to something like $0.40 - $0.60 [48], and speed the whole process up. Perhaps 75% to 90% of transactions currently done manually and on paper should be done electronically. This trend will impact on all educational institutions.

E-commerce practices are also invading education to provide income streams. Many US campuses are now allowing advertising on their web sites – with the income from advertising offsetting the cost of the site. Some universities – such as Georgetown University – have auctioned spare course capacity on the Internet, with bidders hoping, of course, to get a place on an expensive course at a discount.

We can expect eduCommerce to proliferate. Certainly the e-University Business Model assumes that this kind of activity will occur. Nevertheless, entering the e-commerce market has its costs. A Gartner Group report suggests that ecommerce web sites are harder than expected to build, with costs of US$1 million on average – and that this cost is likely to increase by 25% per annum over the next 2 years. Of this cost, 79% is laborrelated, 11% hardware, and 10% software.

Few cost studies of online learning appear to cost the development of the web site at anything like this level of expenditure. This must be a cost in the development of a virtual university. In mixed mode institutions, only part of these costs would now generally relate to the development of an online learning capability. However, the costs of a web site supporting a sophisticated online administrative function are likely to be high.

In general none of the studies undertaken to date adequately factor in the costs of overheads. Although, the costs of putting in equipment directly associated with the projects (e.g., servers) are usually taken into account, as are the costs of software licenses, college operating budgets do not usually reflect the full costs of maintaining networked services. This is something that the US COSTS project is tackling. The annualisation of equipment also causes problems. Most of the cost studies annualise equipment over five years, but in the US in 1998/99 the typical replacement cycle for computers was 3 to 5 years; for central servers 3 to 4 years; and for network electronics, 5 to 6 years. This may seem insignificant – but it impacts on costs significantly, and even more so when the opportunity cost of capital is taken into account.

Replacement costs, which tend to rise, are often underestimated: Ritschard and Spencer argue that the theoretical replacement cost is the average cost per machine times the number of machines to be replaced. They suggest that annual provision for replacement of computers needs to run at 61% of the theoretical replacement cost. Provision for upgrades of equipment that will not be replaced like-for-like requires an additional 8% of the theoretical budget. Another 6% needs to be set aside for unplanned replacements and unforeseen contingencies; a further 20% budgeted for new staff positions; and another 5% for 'out-of-cycle' changes and upgrades.

Finally, higher-level management costs, including planning and evaluation, are rarely taken into account. Overhead management time is often hard to identify. Much depends on the context –the time spent agreeing that a group of enthusiasts can develop a project will be very different to that required to change an institution's direction. Indeed, developing an IT strategy is likely to be expensive.

These omissions are not always obvious from the cost studies. As this section of the paper makes clear, there are both significant costs involved, and the potential for significant savings in administration. The fact that overhead costs and savings are not built into comparative studies of the costs of online, traditional, and other forms of distance education, must mean that any conclusions drawn from such comparative studies have to be treated with care.

E-education Costs and Cost of Other Education Forms

Having looked at the costs involved in online education, let us look at how the costs of e-education courses compare firstly with those of class-based education, and secondly with other forms of distance education.

Costs of face-to-face education

Whether one system is more or less expensive than another will depend upon a range of factors. One approach is to substitute CMC for face-to-face tuition – leaving everything else unchanged. A study conducted at the University of Illinois found that unit costs came down on all nine courses in which asynchronous learning networks were substituted for face-to-face instruction. Bates also thinks that online university courses using just CMC, and involving no real e-materials development, will be cheaper than face-to-face courses . However, most online courses involve some materials, so that cost-efficiency depends on the number of students enrolled.

Bates suggests that a standard Web-based course, with a mix of pre-prepared Web materials, online discussion forums, and print in the form of required texts, is increasingly more cost-effective than face-to-face teaching as numbers per class increase beyond 40 per year over a four-year period. Under 20 students, it is not economically worth doing. Between 20 and 40 students per year per course, any cost differences are likely to be less significant than differences in benefits.

If we widen the argument to take into account training costs that fall on employers, then we find that there are stronger reasons to believe in savings. There is general agreement that online training courses are less expensive that face-to-face ones provided the development costs are spread across sufficient numbers of students (possibly over several years), and provided that one takes into account both savings on travel and accommodation costs, and the fact that less of an employee's productive time is lost (employees now train in their own time rather than in the firm's time).

However, things do not look so good once purpose-built materials are added in: Bates says that if as well as having CMC, one also develops purpose-built materials, then the unit costs will be more expensive than face-to-face tuition. Arizona Learning Systems found that the cost per course enrolment of an 'average' Internet course (US$571) is higher than that of traditional classroom instruction ($474), though labor-for-labor substitution might bring this down to $447. However, much depends on the nature of the materials and their associated development costs which, as we saw, they estimated to vary from US$6000 to $1,000,000 for a three unit Internet course.

Costs of other forms of distance education

What about the cost comparison with other forms of distance education? We have very few studies go on. In an Australian study, Inglis found the online version of a course was less cost efficient at all levels of enrolment than a print-based distance education course.

Elsewhere, Jung compared the costs of presenting standard three credit courses at the Korea National Open University. The course involving textbooks, CD-ROM and electronic tuition was more expensive than the courses using textbooks, radio and face-to-face tuition, or those using textbooks, television and face-to-face tuition. However, dropout was only 10% on the e-course, compared with 60% on the other two types.

Overall, then, these studies suggest that e-education is pushing the costs of distance education up. Some of these additional costs are being passed onto the students, but not all of them. And while no doubt the costs of the technology will come down, the fact remains that those who are not able to afford e-education are being written out of the game. This is true within developed countries, at least in respect of some sectors of the population, but much more widely the case in developing countries.

The output measures used in cost studies vary from study to study. Some studies are based on the cost per student and/or the cost per graduate, but while this may be a suitable measure of output on which to make cost comparisons between educational systems and institutions, for most purposes a better measure is the cost per student per course.

Courses are not, however, standard entities – and hence many studies seek to qualify this measure by defining the kind of course that is being costed in terms of a 'standard' course measured in credit points or credit hours. Unfortunately this also has its problems because internationally the credit weighting of a course may relate to a different things:

(a) the total expected number of hours that the average student will spend studying the course. This measure applies in the UK, for example, where there is an assumption that a standard three year Bachelor's degree will require 120 credit points of study per year, with each credit point being equivalent to something like 10 hours study.

(b) the total timetabled weekly contact hours – which is the system found in the USA – and which of course does not reflect the actual hours study put in by students.

Distance education courses by definition do away with or at least sharply reduce the amount of contact between teachers and students, replacing this with independent study. The latter may be based upon reading, listening to, watching, or otherwise engaging with learning materials: doing assignments and tests; or general reflection. This means that the actual time spent studying the materials may have little relation with the total study time theoretically assigned to the course.

For example, Hülsmann found that the faculty who developed a British Open University course on mathematical modelling estimated that the course would require some 448 hours study over the year – but that the actual time spent studying the various mediated elements of the course was estimated to be 336 hours – so that the course study hours were 1.5 times the media study hours. On the other hand, a course for teachers and social workers offered by NKS Norway required 700 hours study, but only 106 hours of this study arose from the studying the print and video materials provided. Here course hours were 6.8 times the media study hours. These differences leads Hülsmann to suggest that the most appropriate approach to costing media is separately to divide the cost of developing and delivering a given medium by the number of student study hours the medium gives rise to. Thus, for example, a 50 page text that cost £17,500 to develop and that takes an estimated (and average) 5 hours to study has a development cost per student study hour of £350, while a one-hour audiotape that cost £1700 to develop, and takes one hour to study, has a cost per student study hour of £1700.

Although there is an element of subjectivity in estimating how long an (average) student will spend studying a particular element of course material, this does give an easy guide to the relative costs of different media. In practice, however, there is a range of factors that impinge on the costs of developing and delivering media – not least questions related to the quality of the materials and the organisational structure and labor market conditions that underpin its development/ delivery – and these differences are almost certainly behind the range of costs per student study hour that Hülsmann found in practice across the 11 courses that he studied. Having said that, the approach enabled him to show the rough order of costs involved, and to establish beyond reasonable doubt that Internet-based text is more expensive than printed text, with the cheaper media being print and audio.

Low-cost Platform for Web-Based Education

Internet plays a continually increasing role in today''s society. Tele-learning, that is, the application of new information and communication technologies (NICT) to distance learning, is directly affected by these changes. Although the idea of applying computers for educational purposes dates back some 30 years, computer supported education through the use of the Internet seems to be of particular interest. The Web is particularly an interesting technology as it is in an unceasing evolution. It has the ability to combine all these various approaches to learning since the number of students is going beyond university capacity.

Web-based educational systems are asynchronous, that is, they do not require simultaneous presence of teacher and students. Already prepared lectures are available via the Internet through Web browsers or special clients. The front-ends are most often designed in HTML, enriched by Java, JavaScript, or Dynamic HTML. The Web enables worldwide access independent of time, location and unlimited by race, religion and nationalit.

Many developing countries are interested by the advantages and facilities offered by distance learning. For example in T.unisia SUP''COM (Tunis) was developed with the collaboration of INRS Telecommunications (Verdun, Quebec) an interactive virtual environment. The efficiency of the developed platform was evaluated by the implementation of a course concerning the electromagnetic compatibility (EMC) and its application into telecommunications networks. This course has been developed in accordance with needs expressed by Tunisia-Telecom operator in terms of continuing education for its engineers. The distribution of this training course is also programmed for regular registered students at SUP'COM during the academic year 1999-2000.

System Architecture

The particularity of the online distance education, is that, both conception and development phases must take into consideration: The technologic constraints (Bandwidth, client system resources, services availability, *etc*) and pedagogic constraints (course structure, student assistance, homogeneity of the students, *etc*). For that, the procedure for the design and creation of the online course is more difficult and take more time than for a classic course.

To offer a large access to the course, SUP''COM propose two access modes:

a) *Modem access*: In this standard configuration, the connection to the course web-server is achieved by a modem via telephone line. This access mode is useful for far or foreigner students.

b) *Local network access*: This solution is interesting for students who follow the course inside universities campus or companies building.

To facilitate the development of the platform, SUP''COM have studied its logical and physical structure. The logical structure determinate the students way to access to information. With only three layers the students can access to all parts of the environment. The physical structure fixes how site's files were organized in the server. SUP''COM has separated between public and private files and directories.

Another point, the environment is currently under evaluation and it is planned to be a model for other similar online courses, so the structure of the platform must be easy to upgrade, change, modify the course content, integrate other courses, integrate other services. So that, the structure is modular and each module is independent from the others.

Teaching platform development

To develop this platform, SUP''COM has used different Web tools and services for the two following steps:

1. Communication applications development:

To create a familiar environment and to establish contact and communication between student and the tutor, SUP''COM has developed some communication tools: Bottin, CHAT, Mailing list, Conference.

The first one, "Bottin", was created using interaction between HTML pages and database. This software is developed with ASP pages (Active Server Page) whose let us to ask and modify data in a database.

For Conferences, Forum, mailing list and CHAT, SUP''COM has used "O'Reilly Webboard" software. It is a popular Web-based discussion and chat application. It is used in virtual offices and classrooms, corporate intranets, and online forums. It is easy to setup, administer and lets users share information immediately and effortlessly.

2. Course environment development:

The environment is designed as system linking information (text, graphics, sound, video) in a way that allows for easy movement between related documents and sites. Simple, rapid , and can integrate different types of media, SUP''COM has used HTML language to create the site structure.

HTML pages integrate information like indexes, abstracts, *etc* and all are linked to the course documents. The course documents are created using the PDF format (Portable Document Format); This is an interesting format because it produces a very high quality documents, it supports offline and online access modes, it can be viewed by the student navigator or by an external editor. It support document size compression (important thing in case of long courses or multiple course site). It can be generated from all the other documents file formats using Adobe Acrobat software.

SUP''COM has also integrated some animations. These animations were created using Macromedia Flash software. This application support vectorial images and provide highly detailed animations. SUP''COM has used for the web-server operating system, the Windows NT 4.0 Server. It offer the IIS version 4 (Internet Information Server) as HTTP server. With this solution SUP''COM can control, manage, and administer the students account. SUP''COM project also to develop another version of the platform using UNIX as operating system. Then SUP''COM will use PERL, CGI languages for programming the platform's services.

Course site presentation

The environment is composed mainly of Internet sites providing support and services. Each service groups the necessary resources and tools. Resources and tools are implemented and organized according to needs such as communication, assistance, collaboration, documentation, *etc.* Each resource, or generic tool, assumes the presence of a particular system (Forum system, Downloading and Uploading system, Electronic mail system, and many others). The range of services supports all actors of the training during all learning phases. Support is also provided using rubrics for faster access to the information.

1. *Services :* SUP''COM's objective is not to create a simple course in HTML format but to use the Web tools to create a little virtual class in which the student can have a classic student life. To create this environment SUP''COM has implemented different services:

   a) *The bottin*: It is a list that gather all subscribed students. It shows various information about students (name, address, e-mail, *etc*). It facilitate the communication between the different course's actors.

   b) *F.A.Q*: This is a classic web tool that lets the students to have a quickly response to their questions. This list of questions is permanently updated and can contain similar question from other online courses.

   c) *Forum*: this is a virtual space where students can communicate together and with the tutor. Students can send and receive messages, make synchronous ("CHAT") and asynchronous communications. Conferences will be organized at different times to discuss subjects around the course or to take some activities.

d) *File transfer:* This service is provided for who do not know how to use an FTP software. It provides to the students the possibility to upload and download their files to specified directories by simple operations.

e) *Trousse (Pack)*: This service provide student with a pack containing all course documents and a part of the entire Web site. This pack let the student follow the training in offline mode and pass more time in reading the content.

2. *Rubrics*: This part of the site is developed to help and assist the students during the training. It provide various information around the course. These information can be indications about the course content and its different chapters, the training activities, evaluation. SUP''COM implemented the following rubrics:

   a) *Presentation* : This page gives the user a synopsis of the course site and first rules and steps to be followed to begin the training.

   b) *Activities*: This page is intended to give the students idea about all tasks that they have to achieve before evaluation. This part is prepared by the professor.

   c) *Road page:* It is one of the most important elements of the environment. In fact, this page guides the student by the mean of a detailed task planning. The student can take this page as reference during the training. This part is also prepared by the professor because he is able to evaluate the amount of time and effort that each task needs.

d) *Objectives*: In this page the student can find the objectives fixed by the professor in the beginning of the course. By this way, the student can make an auto-evaluation during the course to know if he is in the right direction or not.

e) *The content*: This heading is important in the sense that the student will have a summary of the course content and a presentation of each part. This page lets the student know in advance what kind of knowledge he will have and how to prepare him self.

3. *Course content:* In the site you can find three categories of information:

a) *Pedagogic content:* It is essentially the course content it self. It groups the reading documents, bibliography, links, *etc*. This content integrate in addition to the text, highly detailed graphics, animations and may be sound or video.

b) *Technical content:* It groups all technical information about the platform. The students can use this documentation when they have technical problems. These documents are prepared and maintained by the development team or by the Web site administrator.

c) *General information:* In this part all resources that have an indirect relation with the course can be find.

Index

Adaptive and Intelligent Educational Systems (AIES) 97
Adaptive guidance mechanisms 117
Adaptive Navigation Support (ANS) 96, 108
Asynchronous communication 167

Capital-labor conflict, 13
Computer Mediated Communication (CMC) 92
Counterglobalization 25
Cultural homogenization 1

Dialectical process 6
Diasporic communities, 26
Domain model-based indexing 119

Educational hypermedia systems 108
Educational technology 261

Electro Magnetic Compatibility (EMC) 287
Electronic Textbook (ET) 116
Exploratory learning, 271

Face-toface teaching 274
Feminism 26

General Agreement on Trade in Services (GATS) 2
Global Alliance for Transnational Education (GATE) 127
Globalization 1

Information and communication technologies 180
Innovation Design and Product Development (IDP) 169
Insularism. 11
Intelligent Tutoring Systems (ITS) 97
International human rights organizations 25
International institutions 4
Internet-based distance education 129

Java application 107
Java technology 106

Liberal education 10
Mass education distance teaching 278

Multiculturalism 26
Multimedia technology 194

National Center for Education Statistics (NCES) 127
Neoliberal policies 11
New information and communication technologies (NI 286

Online Learning 269

Postcolonialism 26
Practical Algebra Tutor (PAT) 106

Quality Assurance 5

Telecommunications media 1
Transnational education 3

Web-based,
 applications. 94
 assignment 211
 communication 167
 teaching 92
Web-Based Education (WBE) 89
Web-Based Instructional tools (WBI 90
Web-Based Training (WBT) 191
Web-lecturing technology 201
Workplace organization 8
World Wide Web (WWW) 126